The New Trump Standard

The New Trump Standard

Larry Elder

Creators Publishing
Hermosa Beach, CA

THE NEW TRUMP STANDARD
Copyright © 2019 CREATORS PUBLISHING
All rights reserved. No part of this book may be reproduced or transmitted in any form or by any means, electronic or mechanical, including photocopying, recording or by any information storage and retrieval system, without permission in writing from the author.

Cover art by Peter Kaminski

CREATORS PUBLISHING
737 3rd St
Hermosa Beach, CA 90254
310-337-7003

Although the author and publisher have made every effort to ensure that the information in this book was correct at press time, the author and publisher do not assume and hereby disclaim any liability to any party for any loss, damage or disruption caused by errors or omissions, whether such errors or omissions result from negligence, accident or any other cause.

ISBN (print): 978-1-949673-24-1
ISBN (ebook): 978-1-949673-23-4

First Edition
Printed in the United States of America
1 3 5 7 9 10 8 6 4 2

A Note From the Publisher

Since 1987, Creators has syndicated many of your favorite columns to newspapers. In this digital age, we are bringing collections of those columns to your fingertips. This will allow you to read and reread your favorite columnists, with your own personal digital archive of their work.
—Creators Publishing

Contents

Instead of 'Infrastructure Investment,' How About Killing Davis-Bacon?	1
Where's Hollywood's Apology for Donating to the Clintons While Ignoring Sex Abuse Allegations Against Them?	4
Under the New Trump Standard, Why Wasn't Obama Impeached?	7
The Great S---hole Hypocrisy	10
Had 'News' Media Done Its Job, Obama Would Not Have Become President	13
Take the 'Racist Xenophone' Quiz: Who Said This About Illegal Immigration?	16
What Left-Wing Educators Don't Teach During 'Black History Month'	20
Race and Sports: It's Not 1947 Anymore. Let's Not Pretend That It Is	23
How Many Lives Are Saved by Guns—and Why Don't Gun Controllers Care?	26
Tariffs and Economic Populism: Good Politics, Bad Economics	29
Dem Pundit: 'Paying Off a Porn Star Is Presidential?'	32
No-Drama Obama Versus Trump 'Chaos'	35
Where's the Common Sense in 'Common Sense' Gun Laws?	38
If Laura Ingraham Goes Down for 'Bullying,' You're Next!	41
Why Is Facebook Groveling?	44
Comey Tells Ex-Clinton Aide Stephanopoulos That Trump Is 'Morally Unfit'	47
Joe Biden, Dems and the Race Card: They Don't Leave Home Without It	50
Trump's 2 Big Advantages: Time and Low Expectations	53
Democrats' War on Capitalism	56

Fake Russian Ads Stoked Racial Tensions—Race-Hustling Democrats 'Colluded'	59
In Calling MS-13 Gang Members 'Animals,' Trump Was Kind	62
Roseanne Is Out? Explain Maher, Sharpton and Olbermann	65
Black Motorists Lying on Cops—Who's Doing the 'Racial Profiling'?	68
If Tough Anti-Drug Laws Are 'Racist,' Blame Black Leaders	71
IG Report—Imagine This Level of Bias During the O.J. Simpson Case	74
Criminal Behavior, Not Racism, Explains 'Racial Disparities' in Crime Stats	77
Trump Blamed for Death of Reporters: Did Media Blame Obama for Cop Killers?	80
Slavery: What They Didn't Teach in My High School	83
Russian Bots vs. Media/Academia/Hollywood—Which Had a Bigger Impact on the Election?	86
Trump Skeptical About 'Official Government Findings'? Who Isn't?	89
Anne Hathaway Is Making 'Race Relations' Worse	92
The New York Times Hires Left-Wing Bigot for Its Editorial Board	95
Trump's Hollywood Star Must Go—But They Get a Pass?	98
Trump Haters and Their Double Standards	101
Why Do Ex-Clinton Attack Dogs Davis and Stephanopoulos Get a Pass?	104
Aretha's Funeral: Anti-Trump Bigots Hear Truth About the No. 1 Problem in the Black Community	107
Nike Pays Kaepernick to Push Peddle False, Harmful Narrative of Police Brutality	110
The New York Times' Nikki Haley Smear Vs. The New York Times' G.H.W.B. Smear	113
Ford, Ramirez and a Woman Named Broaddrick	116
'White Male Privilege,' RIP	119
If Kavanaugh Is 'Partisan,' Should We Impeach Justice	122

RBG?	
Chris Matthews' Reaction to Kanye West Exposes the Left's Race-Card Hustle	125
The 'Voter ID Is Racist' Con	128
Pittsburgh Synagogue Massacre: Obama Slams 'Hateful Rhetoric'—Did He Mean Trump's, or His Own?	131
Midterms: Republicans Had a Great Story to Tell—and It Staved Off Disaster	134
If Trump Is 'Racist,' He Needs to Go Back to Racism School	137
Don't Let Trump Hatred Thwart the School Choice Movement	140
On Immigration, Hillary Clinton and John Kerry Discover Their Inner Trump	143
Fake Praise for GHWB: Where Were Media When He Needed Them?	146
Mueller Probe: If Convictions Equals Success, Whitewater Was a Triumph	149
Gov. Jerry 'Moonbeam' Brown's Warning to Fellow Democrats	152
About the Author	155

Instead of 'Infrastructure Investment,' How About Killing Davis-Bacon?

January 4, 2018

Is there a difference between President Barack Obama's "stimulus" and President Donald Trump's "infrastructure investment"? Despite costing $800 billion, most economists do not believe Obama's "stimulus" program did much stimulating. During the Great Depression, President Franklin Roosevelt's secretary of Treasury wrote in his diary that the New Deal spending, designed to rescue the economy, was not working. Treasury Secretary Henry Morgenthau wrote: "We have tried spending money. We are spending more than we have ever spent before and it does not work. ... I want to see this country prosperous. I want to see people get a job. I want to see people get enough to eat. We have never made good on our promises. ... I say after eight years of this Administration we have just as much unemployment as when we started and an enormous debt to boot!"

Trump, in announcing his upcoming plans for 2018, said: "Infrastructure is, by far, the easiest. People want it, Republicans and Democrats. We're going to have tremendous Democrat support on infrastructure, as you know. I could've started with infrastructure. I actually wanted to save the easy one for the one down the road. We'll be having that done pretty quickly."

What if, instead of spending more on infrastructure, the government began paying nearly 20 percent less for projects? And how about pushing privatization, where possible, over the inevitably more costly government spending?

The Davis-Bacon Act, a Depression-era measure, was designed to thwart black workers from competing against white workers. It requires federal contractors to pay "prevailing union wages." This act sought to shut out black workers from competing for construction jobs after white workers protested that Southern blacks were hired to build a Veterans Bureau hospital in Long Island, New York—the district of Rep. Robert Bacon, one of the bill's sponsors. It is remarkable the Davis-Bacon still lives despite its racist intent and its discriminatory effect—to this day—on black workers. Passed in 1931, two Republicans teamed up to sponsor it.

In a labor market dominated by exclusionary unions that demanded above-market wages, blacks, at the time, competed by working for less money than the unionists. Davis-Bacon stopped this by requiring federal contractors to pay prevailing local union wages, causing massive black unemployment. Lawmakers made no secret of the law's goal.

In the House of Representatives, Congressman William Upshaw, D-Ga., said: "You will not think that a Southern man is more than human if he smiles over the fact of your reaction to that real problem you are confronted with in any community with a superabundance or large aggregation of Negro labor." Rep. Miles Clayton Allgood, D-Ala., supported the bill and complained of "cheap colored labor" that "is in competition with white labor throughout the country." Rep. John J. Cochran, D-Mo., stated that he had "received numerous complaints in recent months about Southern contractors employing low-paid colored mechanics getting work and bringing the employees from the South."

Davis-Bacon adds as much as 20 percent more to the cost of any federal project. And most states have enacted local Davis-Bacon laws that similarly jack up the price of those government construction projects.

This brings us to privatization. Why not encourage more projects to be built and run by the private market?

In California, for example, the Democratic governor pushes a "bullet train" that promises to benefit Los Angeles-to-San Francisco travelers. Yet the governor expects taxpayers to pay for at least part of this supposedly wonderful project. If it is predicted to be so profitable, why should taxpayers finance it?

Finally, it is not true that our gas tax has not kept pace with federal highway route expenses. From 1982 through 2014, federal gas tax revenues increased nearly 6 percent a year, according to the Cato Institute's Chris Edwards. He also points out that, beyond transportation and water, "most of America's infrastructure is provided by the private sector, not governments." "In fact," says Edwards, "private infrastructure spending—on factories, freight rail, cell towers, pipelines, refineries, and other items—is four times larger than federal, state, and local government infrastructure spending combined."

Businessman Trump is uniquely positioned to make the case not for more government spending but for less—but more efficient—spending. Obama's failed "stimulus" should serve as Exhibit A for what we ought not do. Trump should make the case to abolish Davis-Bacon, and for the privatization of as much infrastructure as possible.

So what's the difference between Obama's "stimulus" and Trump's "infrastructure investment"? Obama spent $830 billion in four years, while Trump says he wants to spend as much as $1 trillion in 10 years. Unless we kill Davis-Bacon and move toward more privatization, the answer may be no difference at all.

Where's Hollywood's Apology for Donating to the Clintons While Ignoring Sex Abuse Allegations Against Them?

January 11, 2018

In President Donald Trump era, Hollywood has become more political and less entertaining, while Washington, D.C., has become more entertaining and less political. The theme of this year's Golden Globes awards show was "Time's Up," the movement to salute the women who have come forward to tell their stories of sexual abuse, assault or harassment in the workplace.

Actress Reese Witherspoon said, "I want to thank everyone who broke their silence this year and spoke up about abuse and harassment. You are so brave. ... So people out there who are feeling silenced by harassment, discrimination, abuse: Time is up. We see you, we hear you, and we will tell your stories."

But for years women have publicly told their stories of sexual abuse and rape by Bill Clinton. One alleged rape survivor, Juanita Broaddrick, claims that Hillary Clinton attempted to verbally threaten her into silence about two weeks after Broaddrick's alleged rape by Bill Clinton. The Hollywood community raised millions of dollars for the Clintons, despite Broaddrick's accusation and the accusations of sexual harassment and battery by Paula Jones and Kathleen Willey. It's hard to get much more public than telling your story on "60 Minutes" and "Dateline NBC," as did Willey and Broaddrick, respectively.

Yet this did not disturb the Hollywood community.

Nor is the "Time's Up" Hollywood community bothered by how it treats *conservative* females. HBO's Bill Maher, who contributed $1 million to a Democratic super political action committee, called former Republican vice presidential candidate Sarah Palin both the C-word and a "dumb t---" (a derisive slang word for female genitalia). He also referred to Palin and former Minnesota congresswoman Michele Bachmann, who ran as a Republican presidential candidate in 2012, as "two bimbos." If any guests, female or male, canceled appearances or refused to appear on Maher's show until he apologized for his vulgar insults of conservative woman, it did not make news.

In three hours of the Golden Globes' celebration of the empowerment of women, neither host Seth Meyers nor Oprah Winfrey, who was given a special award for "outstanding contributions to the world of entertainment," nor any presenter or winner found time to say something, *anything*, about the abuse and oppression of women in the Muslim and Arab world. Not one word.

Actress Debra Messing, on the red carpet before the show started, made it clear that "Time's Up" meant "equal pay." She said: "Time is up. We want diversity. We want intersectional gender parity, we want equal pay." Messing told the E! host who was interviewing her: "I was so shocked to hear that E! doesn't believe in paying their female co-hosts the same as their male co-hosts. ... We want people to start having this conversation that women are just as valuable as men. Fifteen million dollars has been raised for funds for advocacy and legal representation for women. ... This is not about Hollywood. This is about every woman in every industry globally. As someone in *this* industry, we need equal representation. We want 50/50 by 2020. And within that 50 percent, 30 percent women of color."

Really? So until and unless every industry is 50 percent female and 30 percent of those women of color, we suffer from racial and sex discrimination? So 50 percent of physicists must be female and 30 percent of them women of color? Secretaries? Ditch diggers? Supermodels? NBA players? Ballerinas?

Actress Natalie Portman, in announcing the nominees for best director, cheapened the award and simultaneously took a swipe at men, saying, "And here are the *all-male* nominees." How do you think that made the winner, Guillermo del Toro, feel? After all, he only won the award, implied Portman, against a sexist fraternity that shuts out more-deserving women.

How a little perspective on this "female empowerment" business? There are more women in college then men. In recent years, an average of 50 percent of the entering medical school and law school classes are female. And young women out-earn young men. When you examine the apples to apples data, comparing women with the same level and type of education and work experience to their male counterparts, there's virtually no difference in the incomes of these similarly situated men and women.

One more thing about the Golden Globes show and the attendees' hostility toward President Trump. Hollywood is an industry heavily represented by Jews. It is an industry that gave us masterpieces like "Schindler's List." Yet not one person on Sunday night, Jew or gentile, gave Trump an "Atta boy" for moving our embassy from Tel Aviv to Jerusalem, something even Barack Obama promised but failed to do.

Will one, just one, A-list actor or actress say something positive about President Donald Trump? What does it say about Hollywood's alleged open-mindedness and tolerance that such a thing would be a career-ending act of courage? On the other hand, Sharon Stone looked great. And—to avoid accusations of sexism—so did Tom Hanks.

Under the New Trump Standard, Why Wasn't Obama Impeached?

January 28, 2018

In the era of President Donald Trump, Democrats think presidents should be impeached over policy differences.

In Trump's case, the Democrats accuse him of winning the election by "colluding" with Russia to win. After nearly a year of investigations, there does not appear to be any evidence. Yet many Democrats have already called for impeachment.

In truth, Democrats want this President out because they don't like him or his policies. One of Trump's major campaign promises was to build a "wall" to protect our southern border. Never mind that, in 2006, 26 Democratic senators—including Hillary Clinton, then-Sen. Barack Obama and Chuck Schumer—voted for hundreds of miles of barriers and fencing. And every Senate Democrat voted for 2013's Border Security, Economic Opportunity, and Immigration Modernization Act, which again called for hundreds of miles of barriers.

But Trump is "racist" and "xenophobic." Rep. Al Green, D-Texas, calls Trump a "bigot in the White House who incites hatred and hostility," which, says Green, is a "high misdemeanor" that constitutes an impeachable offense.

All right, let's apply the Democrats' new standard for impeachment to President Obama and his decision in 2011 to pull all the troops from Iraq against the advice of his national security team. President George W. Bush warned his successor. Bush turned around the Iraq War with his controversial "surge," a troop increase of about 21,500 in 2007. Former Vice President Dick Cheney, in October 2011, two months before Obama pulled out all the troops in Iraq, said that Bush's 2007 agreement envisioned a negotiation for a stay-behind force: "There was another provision in (Bush's status-of-forces agreement) that's very important, seems to have been ignored, which was that we would also reserve the right to negotiate with the Iraqis on some stay-behind forces. ... They're a new democracy; they're not very well-organized yet. I worry that in the rush for the exit here, that we may in fact make it very difficult for them to succeed."

But then-Sen. Barack Obama, who called the Iraq War "dumb," not only opposed Bush's surge but also predicted it would make things worse: "I am not persuaded that 20,000 additional troops in Iraq is going to solve the sectarian violence there. In fact, I think it will do the reverse. ... So I am going to actively oppose the President's proposal."

But the surge did work. By 2008, the violence subsided to the point where American soldiers, celebrating with Iraqis in Ramadi, were on the streets not even wearing their helmets. War correspondent Dexter Filkins, who had all but given up in Iraq when he was last there just two years earlier, could not believe the improvement: "The progress here is remarkable," said Filkins in 2008. "I came back to Iraq after being away for nearly two years, and honestly, parts of it are difficult for me to recognize. The park out in front of the house where I live—on the Tigris River—was a dead, dying, spooky place. It's now filled with people—families with children, women walking alone, even at night. That was inconceivable in 2006. The Iraqis who are out there walking in the parks were making their own judgments—that it is safe enough for them to go out for a walk. They're voting with their feet. It's a wonderful thing to see." But Filkins warned that the gains could erode. "It's pretty clear," Filkins said, "that the calm is very fragile. The calm is built on a series of arrangements that are not self-sustaining; indeed, some of which, like the Sunni Awakening, are showing signs of coming apart. So the genie is back in the bottle, but I'm not sure for how long."

Obama, however, pulled out all the troops *against* the advice given by Obama's CIA chief, his secretary of defense, the United States ambassador to Iraq, his national security adviser, the Joint Chiefs of Staff and then-Secretary of State Hillary Clinton. This commander in chief with no military experience rejected the apparent unanimous advice from his defense team: Leave a stay-behind force or run the risk of terrorists filling the power vacuum.

But Obama did not listen.

As to the Joint Chiefs' opposition to what became known as the "Iraq bug-out," now-retired Army Chief of Staff Gen. Ray Odierno said: "I go back to the work we did in 2007 (through) 2010, and we got into a place that was really good. Violence was low, the economy was growing, politics looked like it was heading in the right direction. ... We thought we had it going exactly in the right direction, but now we watch it fall apart. It's frustrating. ... I think, maybe, if we had stayed a little more engaged, I think maybe it might have prevented it."

If policy disagreement is the new standard for impeachment in the Trump era, wouldn't Obama's Iraq bug-out qualify?

The Great S---hole Hypocrisy

January 25, 2018

Breaking news: President Donald Trump uses profanity.

When Trump's apparent use of the word "s---hole" makes headlines, one cannot help but recall the analysis of the media provided by President Obama's deputy national security adviser and foreign policy speechwriter. In discussing his perception of reporters' ignorance of foreign affairs, Ben Rhodes said: "Most of the outlets are reporting on world events from Washington. The average reporter we talk to is 27 years old, and their only reporting experience consists of being around political campaigns. That's a sea change. They literally know nothing."

Presidents curse.

President Lyndon Baines Johnson taped himself cursing and using racial epithets. President Richard Nixon taped himself cursing, using racial epithets and making anti-Semitic comments. Then-presidential candidate George W. Bush was caught on a hot mic calling reporter Adam Clymer a "major-league a--hole from The New York Times." Former ABC reporter Ann Compton says that on at least two occasions, President Barack Obama launched into off-the-record "tirades" against the media. In one case, Compton described the President's scolding as "profanity laced."

But in Trump's case, critics claim his recent use of profanity corroborates, underscores and advances the narrative that the President is "racist." Here's what happened. In a "bi-partisan" White House discussion about the immigration debate, Trump reportedly referred to Haiti and African countries as "s---holes," and wondered why America takes in more immigrants from Africa than from countries like Norway.

Out came the pitchforks. One Democrat, Texas Rep. Al Green, not only pronounced the President "racist," but says that his alleged racism constitutes grounds for impeachment, apart from the findings of the special counsel.

What about President Obama?

He, too, made a Trump-like statement about the cultural superiority of one group over another. In April 2016, The Atlantic published an article about President Obama's foreign policy challenges, a frustrated Obama complained about the difficulty of achieving peace in the Middle East. Obama said, "If only everyone [in the Middle East] could be like Scandinavians, this [achieving peace] would all be easy."

Note to Rep. Green: Norway is Scandinavian country. Again, Obama made *the same point* as did Trump—yet no one called Obama "racist."

Obama also called Libya, an African country, a "s--- show" following his admittedly failed military intervention in 2011. He blamed its tribal divisions: "The degree of tribal division in Libya was greater than our analysts had expected. And our ability to have any kind of structure there that we could interact with and start training and start providing resources broke down very quickly."

Republican Sen. Lindsey Graham used harsh language in describing countries to our south. Graham, in 2013, said: "The people coming across the southern border live in hellholes. They don't like that. They want to come here. Our problem is we can't have everybody in the world who lives in a hellhole come to America." Where were the racism-watchers then?

Few Trump-haters appear to have read "The Dark Side of Camelot" by former New York Times writer Seymour Hersh. He writes that President John F. Kennedy was warned about a wealthy, high-profile Democrat, who not only supported another candidate but tried to get evidence of Kennedy's alleged extra-marital liaisons. Later, when some Senators pushed for a high-profile ambassadorship for this Democratic donor, Kennedy did not forget. "I'm going to f--- him," Kennedy said. "I'm going to send him to one of those boogie republics in Central Africa." "Boogie republics" does not sound like a term of endearment.

Then there's Kennedy's treatment of Sammy Davis Jr. The gifted singer/actor/dancer/musician/comedian campaigned hard for JFK in the 1960 presidential race, and even postponed his wedding to a white actress until after the election. Davis feared his marriage might alienate voters who disapproved of interracial marriage, so he waited until after

Kennedy won to get married. But after Kennedy got elected, the newly married Sammy was *uninvited* to Kennedy's inauguration, to appease those offended by the high-profile marriage.

As for Trump's "racism," he must be putting forth policies to harm blacks, right? But Trump seeks to empower urban parents through education vouchers so that parents can opt out of an underperforming public school. Trump wants to stop illegal immigration. Economists like Harvard's Jorge Borjas claim that urban American workers without high school diplomas face competition for jobs against unskilled illegal workers, who also put downward pressure on the wages of these U.S. workers.

In an era where activists unfairly brand police as racist profilers, Trumps supports the cops. The bogus Black Lives Matter movement has caused an increase in murder and other types of violent crime in cities like St. Louis, (right outside Ferguson) and Baltimore. The victims of this increased crime are disproportionately black—the very people the activists purport to care about. In one year of the Trump administration, blacks have seen an increase in the labor force participation rate and blacks are enjoying record low levels of unemployment.

If Trump wants to practice racism, his incompetence has been staggering.

Had 'News' Media Done Its Job, Obama Would Not Have Become President

February 1, 2018

A photojournalist withheld publication of a 2005 photograph of a smiling then-Sen. Barack Obama with a beaming Louis Farrakhan, the anti-Semitic, anti-white leader of the Nation of Islam.

The occasion was a meeting with the Congressional Black Caucus. The photographer, Askia Muhammad, said that almost immediately after he took the picture a CBC staffer called and said, "We have to have the picture back." Muhammad later surrendered the disk with the photo to Farrakhan's chief of staff. "I gave the picture up at the time and basically swore secrecy," Muhammad said in an interview with the Trice Edney News Wire. "But after the (presidential) nomination was secured and all the way up until the inauguration; then for eight years after he was President, it was kept under cover."

Why this concern in 2005 when then-Sen. Obama, just elected, had not announced his plan to run for the presidency? The Jerusalem Post writes: "As there was already talk in 2005 of Obama running for president, Muhammad said he and others did not want to harm the Democrat's chances. It isn't clear who was employing Muhammad at the time, but he had previously worked for the Nation of Islam publication, The Final Call."

Would the photo have mattered? Could it have derailed Obama's chance to become president?

Harvard Law School professor emeritus and lifelong liberal Alan Dershowitz says he would not have campaigned for Obama had he been aware of this photograph. Dershowitz says: "Louis Farrakhan is a virulent anti-Semite. He's called Judaism a 'gutter religion.' He's anti-American. He is a horrible, horrible human being.

"And if I had known that the President had posed smilingly with (Farrakhan) when he was a senator, I would not have campaigned for Barack Obama. It would have influenced my decision. Look, I threatened to leave the Democratic Party if Keith Ellison were elected as chairman because of his association with Farrakhan. You don't associate with a bigot. You don't associate with an anti-Semite."

The suppression of the Obama-Farrakhan photo is just the latest example of the degree to which Obama benefited from extraordinarily special treatment.

Obama's longtime association with the Rev. Jeremiah Wright of Chicago's Trinity United Church of Christ would likely have derailed his candidacy had media pounced on this as they did the Trump "Access Hollywood" tape. But for Fox News' coverage of Wright and the videotapes of his fiery sermons, the other major media would have avoided or downplayed Obama's 20-year association with a pastor who gave fiery sermons critical of America and who had a longtime friendship with Farrakhan.

Ezra Klein, then with The Washington Post, set up a private internet forum he called JournoList, which served as an online gathering place for several hundred like-minded (aka liberal) reporters. When the Jeremiah Wright scandal broke, several reporters on the "J-List" literally schemed of ways to deflect attention from the scandal. About JournoList, Obama and Wright, the Daily Caller wrote: "In one instance, Spencer Ackerman of the Washington Independent urged his colleagues to deflect attention from Obama's relationship with Wright by changing the subject. Pick one of Obama's conservative critics, Ackerman wrote, 'Fred Barnes, Karl Rove, who cares—and call them racists.'"

Then there's the Los Angeles Times, which, to this day, has not and will not publish even a transcript of the "Khalidi tapes." Rashid Khalidi, an Obama friend and a University of Chicago Palestinian-American professor of Middle East studies, had a going-away party to celebrate his new post at Columbia University. Someone gave the Los Angeles Times a videotape of this 2003 event that Obama attended, where he reminisced about their friendship in a tribute to the professor.

Khalidi was an outspoken supporter of Yasser Arafat and the Palestinian Liberation Organization. But what he said and what others said at this farewell party, we will never know. Were attendees bashing

Israel? Did Obama bash Israel? The Times says it promised the unnamed source who provided the videotape not to air or reproduce the tape. The paper, whose editorial board endorsed Obama, claims it simply kept its promise to a source. If a tape could have ended Trump's 2016 campaign, would the LA Times, whose editorial board twice endorsed Obama and considered Trump a danger to the world, have sat on it?

Joan Walsh of the liberal website Salon.com described how fellow journalists were "swooning" during the presidential candidacy over the first-time senator from Illinois. "I was struck," Walsh said, "when I got to Iowa and New Hampshire in January, by how our media colleagues were just swooning over Barack Obama. That is not too strong a word. They were *swooning* (emphasis added). I was at a speech. ... The biggest names in our business were there. ... They could repeat some of his speech lines to one another. It was like a Bruce Springsteen concert where the fans sing along."

Still, Trump won. Amazing.

Take the 'Racist Xenophobe' Quiz: Who Said This About Illegal Immigration?

February 8, 2018

Which alleged "racist xenophobe" made these statements about illegal immigration?

"Those who enter the country illegally and those who employ them disrespect the rule of law, and they are showing disregard for those who are following the law. We simply cannot allow people to pour into the United States undetected, undocumented (and) unchecked, and circumventing the line of people who are waiting patiently, diligently and lawfully to become immigrants in this country."

A) Adolf Hitler
B) Donald Trump
C) Barack Obama

Answer: Then-Sen. Obama, news conference, 2005

"Our administration has moved aggressively to secure our borders more by hiring a record number of new border guards, by deporting twice as many criminal aliens as ever before, by cracking down on illegal hiring, by barring welfare benefits to illegal aliens."

A) Joseph Stalin
B) Donald Trump
C) Bill Clinton

Answer: President Clinton, State of the Union address, 1995

"If making it easy to be an illegal alien isn't enough, how about offering an award to be an illegal immigrant. No sane country would do that, right? Guess again."

A) Jack the Ripper
B) Donald Trump
C) Sen. Harry Reid, D-Nev.

Answer: Reid, Senate floor, 1993

"In approaching immigration reform, I believe we must enact tough, practical reforms that ensure and promote the legal and orderly entry of immigrants into our country."

A) Idi Amin
B) Donald Trump
C) Barack Obama

Answer: Sen. Obama, Senate floor, 2007

"We all agree on the need to better secure the border, and to punish employers who choose to hire illegal immigrants."

A) Pol Pot
B) Donald Trump
C) Barack Obama

Answer: Sen. Obama, 2005

"All Americans, not only in the states most heavily affected but in every place in this country, are rightly disturbed by the large numbers of illegal aliens entering our country. The jobs they hold might otherwise be held by citizens or legal immigrants. The public services they use impose burdens on our taxpayers."

A) Michael Myers
B) Donald Trump
C) Bill Clinton

Answer: President Clinton, State of the Union address, 1995

"We will try to do more to speed the deportation of illegal aliens who are arrested for crimes, to better identify illegal aliens in the workplace."

A) Jeffrey Dahmer
B) Donald Trump
C) Bill Clinton

Answer: President Clinton, State of the Union address, 1995

"I continue to believe that we need stronger enforcement on the border and at the workplace. And that means a workable mandatory system that employers must use to verify the legality of their workers."

A) Kim Jong Un
B) Donald Trump
C) Barack Obama

Answer: Sen. Obama, Senate floor, 2007

"If you break our laws by entering this country without permission and give birth to a child, we reward that child with U.S. citizenship and guarantee full access to all public and social services this society provides—and that's a lot of services. Is it any wonder that two-thirds of babies born at taxpayer expense (in) county-run hospitals in Los Angeles are born to illegal alien mothers?"

A) Kim Kardashian
B) Donald Trump
C) Harry Reid

Answer: Sen. Reid, Senate floor, 1993

"We need to start by giving agencies charged with border security new technology, new facilities and more people to stop, process and deport illegal immigrants."

A) Rasputin
B) Donald Trump
C) Barack Obama

Answer: Sen. Barack Obama, 2005

"Right now we've got millions of illegal immigrants who live and work here without knowing their identity or background."

A) Freddy Krueger
B) Donald Trump
C) Barack Obama

Answer: Sen. Obama, 2005

"We are a nation of immigrants. But we are also a nation of laws. It is wrong and ultimately self-defeating for a nation of immigrants to permit the kind of abuse of our immigration laws we have seen in recent years, and we must do more to stop it."

A) Vlad the Impaler
B) Donald Trump
C) Bill Clinton

Answer: President Clinton, State of the Union address, 1995

"Let me repeat: We need strong border security at the borders."

A) Hassan Nasrallah
B) Donald Trump
C) Barack Obama

Answer: Barack Obama, 2005

"If only everyone (in the Middle East) could be like Scandinavians, (achieving peace) would all be easy."
A) Al Capone
B) Donald Trump
C) Barack Obama
Answer: President Obama, 2016

"There are too many (migrants) now. ... Europe, for example, Germany, cannot become an Arab country. Germany is Germany. ... From a moral point of view, too, I think refugees should only be admitted temporarily."
A) Joseph Goebbels
B) Donald Trump
C) Dalai Llama
Answer: Dalai Llama, 2016

Not long ago, both Democrats and Republicans advocated safe, secure borders and an immigration policy of admitting immigrants who benefit, not burden, Americans. Que paso?

What Left-Wing Educators Don't Teach During 'Black History Month'

February 15, 2018

When will Black History Month be ... history?

Apart from the bizarre notion that educators should set aside one month to salute the historical achievements of one race apart from and above the historical achievements of other races, Black History Month appears to omit a lot of black history.

About slavery, do our mostly left-wing educators teach that slavery was not unique to America and is as old as humankind? As economist and author Thomas Sowell says: "More whites were brought as slaves to North Africa than blacks brought as slaves to the United States or to the 13 colonies from which it was formed. White slaves were still being bought and sold in the Ottoman Empire, decades after blacks were freed in the United States."

Are students taught that "race-based preferences," sometimes called "affirmative action," were *opposed* by several civil rights leaders? While National Urban League Executive Director Whitney Young supported a type of "Marshall Plan" for a period of 10 years to make up for historical discrimination, his board of directors refused to endorse the plan. In rejecting it, the president of the Urban League in Pittsburgh said the public would ask, "What in blazes are these guys up to? They tell us for years that we must buy (nondiscrimination) and then they say, 'It isn't what we want.'" A member of the Urban League in New York objected to what he called "the heart of it—the business of employing Negroes (because they are Negroes)." Bayard Rustin was one of Martin Luther King Jr.'s key lieutenants and helped to plan and organize the civil rights march in D.C. that culminated in King's famous "I Have a

Dream" speech. Rustin, an openly gay black man, also opposed race-based preferences.

Do our left-wing educators, during Black History Month, note that President Franklin Delano Roosevelt's celebrated New Deal actually *hurt* blacks? According to Cato Institute's Jim Powell, blacks lost as many as 500,000 jobs as a result of anti-competitive, job-killing regulations of the New Deal. Powell writes: "The flagship of the New Deal was the National Industrial Recovery Act, passed in June 1933. It authorized the president to issue executive orders establishing some 700 industrial cartels, which restricted output and forced wages and prices above market levels. The minimum wage regulations made it illegal for employers to hire people who weren't worth the minimum because they lacked skills. As a result, some 500,000 blacks, particularly in the South, were estimated to have lost their jobs. Marginal workers, like unskilled blacks, desperately needed an expanding economy to create more jobs. Yet New Deal policies made it harder for employers to hire people. FDR tripled federal taxes between 1933 and 1940. ... By giving labor unions the monopoly power to exclusively represent employees in a workplace, the (1935) Wagner Act had the effect of excluding blacks, since the dominant unions discriminated against blacks."

Are students taught that gun control, widely embraced by today's black leadership, began as a means to deny free blacks the right to own guns? In ruling that blacks were chattel property in the Dred Scott case, Supreme Court Chief Justice Roger Taney warned of that the consequences of ruling otherwise would mean that blacks would be able to own guns. If blacks were "entitled to the privileges and immunities of citizens," said Taney, "it would give persons of the Negro race, who were recognized as citizens in any one state of the union, the right ... to keep and carry arms wherever they went ... endangering the peace and safety of the state."

Are students taught that generations of civil rights leaders *opposed* immigration—both legal and illegal immigration? After the Civil War, black abolitionist Frederick Douglass implored employers to hire blacks over new immigrants. Twenty-five years later, Booker T. Washington pleaded with Southern industrialists to hire blacks over new immigrants: "One third of the population of the South is of the Negro race. ... To those of the white race who look to the incoming of those of foreign birth and strange tongue and habits for the prosperity of the South: Cast down your bucket where you are. Cast it down among the eight millions of Negroes whose habits you know, whose fidelity and love you have tested in days when to have proved treacherous meant the ruin of your fireside."

About illegal immigration, an issue that nearly all of the today's so-called black leaders simply ignore, Coretta Scott King signed a letter urging Congress to retain harsh sanctions against employers who knowingly hire illegal workers. The letter said: "We are concerned ... that ... the elimination of employer sanctions will cause another problem—the revival of the pre-1986 discrimination against black and brown U.S. and documented workers, in favor of cheap labor—the undocumented workers. This would undoubtedly exacerbate an already severe economic crisis in communities where there are large numbers of new immigrants."

These are just a few historical and inconvenient notes left on the cutting room floor during Black History Month.

Race and Sports: It's Not 1947 Anymore. Let's Not Pretend That It Is

February 22, 2018

ESPN recently re-aired a three-part documentary about the long rivalry between two storied NBA basketball teams, the Los Angeles Lakers and the Boston Celtics, and their two marquee players, Magic Johnson and Larry Bird, respectively.

After another devastating Laker loss, this time in the 1984 finals, Laker star Magic Johnson said he felt so disappointed, in part, because he let down blacks. So many black fans were pulling for him, including, he discovered, many black residents of Boston.

As a Los Angeles native, I, too, wanted the Lakers to win. But how did the Lakers of the era become the "black team" and how did the Bird-led team become the "white team"? Sure, the Celtics were led by Bird—a white player—but the Celtics' coach, K.C. Jones, was black, as were several key players, including guards Dennis Johnson and Gerald Henderson, as well as center Robert Parrish and forward Cedric "Cornbread" Maxwell. Meanwhile, the Lakers' head coach was Pat Riley, a white man.

No doubt many whites pulled for Bird because he's white. As a white friend and Larry Bird fan once told me, "White people have pride, too." And no doubt that many black people pulled for Magic Johnson over Bird because Johnson is black. Who cares? Something can be *racial* without being *racist*. One black Celtic player said it bothered him that some blacks considered him to be playing for a "white team." But another black player, M.L. Carr, said he could not have cared less about the black-versus-white nonsense and just wanted to beat Los Angeles.

It's also worth noting that Bird never played into the "Great White Hope" nonsense. When an opposing ballplayer, Isiah Thomas, suggested that if Bird were a black player he "would be just another good guy," Bird did not take the bait. He could have fired back and accused the black player of racism. But he wanted nothing to do with what he perceived as a media-made controversy. When the player apologized, Bird accepted it, and that was that. Bird said: "The main thing is that if the statement doesn't bother me, it shouldn't bother anybody. If Isiah tells me it was a joking matter, it should be left at that. The NBA is sometimes not the easiest thing to be in, and after a game like that, in the heat of the locker room, it's probably not the best time to talk to us. I've answered a lot of questions about it, and talked about it to my family, and they still love Isiah Thomas."

Now how about a little perspective?

In 1950, the first black player entered the NBA. The '60s saw the breakout of black superstars like Bill Russell, Wilt Chamberlain, Oscar Robertson, Elgin Baylor, Walt Bellamy, Hal Greer and many more. Fast-forward to today. As of 2017, 75 percent of the roughly 500 players in the NBA are black. Of the 30 coaches in the NBA, eight of them—27 percent—are black.

Jackie Robinson, the first black baseball player in the modern major leagues, said, he, too, felt pressured to live up to the expectations of black America. He had good reason. There were zero blacks playing in the major leagues at the time he entered in 1947. There was a belief among many whites, and probably blacks, too, that black ballplayers just could not compete against whites. *That's* pressure.

Robinson faced hostility from teammates and opponents, many of whom attempted to physically harm him while playing. At that time, pre-television, baseball—along with boxing and horse racing—occupied a much bigger stage for the attention of the American public. Excruciating pressure was on Robinson, because what he represented and what he meant to millions of black Americans transcended baseball.

Because of pioneers like Jackie Robinson, we can now pretty much sit back and just watch a good game. Politics can wait a few hours.

During their playing days, Johnson and Bird became good friends. Since their playing days, their friendship has deepened. Bird even stunned Celtics fans when, after a tough loss, Bird—during the post-game press conference—conceded that Johnson was "the best I've ever seen." Turns out, when the noise died down, Bird just wanted to beat

Johnson, whom he respected as a player and as a man. Johnson just wanted to beat Bird, whom he respected as a player and as a man. And that's how it should be.

How Many Lives Are Saved by Guns—and Why Don't Gun Controllers Care?

March 1, 2018

Lost in the current debate about gun control are three important points.

First, how many lives are *saved* each year through the use of firearms. We know that for the last several years, according to the Centers for Disease Control (which tracks all U.S. deaths by cause), roughly 11,000 lives have been lost through non-suicide deaths involving a firearm each year.

Why ignore gun suicides?

Following the 1994 Brady Handgun Violence Prevention Act's imposition of a five-day waiting period for the 32 states previously not subject to such waiting periods, gun control supporters expected those states would have seen a reduction in crime, compared with the other 18 "control" states. But according to The Journal of the American Medical Association: "Our analyses provide no evidence that implementation of the Brady Act was associated with a reduction in homicide rates. ... We find no differences in homicide or firearm homicide rates to adult victims in the 32 states directly subject to the Brady Act provisions compared with the remaining control states." The study *did* find a decrease in gun suicides for men over 55. But the overall suicide rate remained unchanged. Men over 55 simply resorted to other means to kill themselves.

As for determining how many lives are saved by guns, regulations bar the CDC from conducting original research of the defensive use of firearms. But after the Sandy Hook school massacre in 2012, President Barack Obama issued an executive order allowing the agency to review existing studies on causes of and ways to reduce gun violence. As to defensives uses of guns, the CDC report said, "Studies that directly assessed the effect of actual defensive uses of guns (i.e., incidents in which a gun was 'used' by the crime victim in the sense of attacking or threatening an offender) have found consistently lower injury rates among gun-using crime victims compared with victims who used other self-protective strategies. ... Almost all national survey estimates indicate that defensive gun uses by victims are at least as common as offensive uses by criminals, with estimates of annual uses ranging from about 500,000 to more than 3 million per year, in the context of about 300,000 violent crimes involving firearms in 2008."

Criminologist and researcher Gary Kleck, using his own commissioned phone surveys and number extrapolation, estimates that Americans use guns for defensive purposes 1.2 million times each year—and that 1 in 6 Americans who have used guns defensively believe someone would have died but for their ability to resort to their defensive use of firearms. Twenty years ago economist John Lott, author of "More Guns, Less Crime," and his research partner wrote: "We find that allowing citizens to carry concealed weapons deters violent crimes and it appears to produce no increase in accidental deaths. If those states which did not have right-to-carry concealed gun provisions had adopted them in 1992, approximately 1,570 murders; 4,177 rapes; and over 60,000 aggravated assaults would have been avoided yearly."

The second point, often ignored, is the very purpose of the Second Amendment. It is to prevent government tyranny through the power of a citizens' militia. Since many on the left denounce President Donald Trump as a "tyrant" or a "dictator" or a "Hitler," they might find that the Second Amendment could come in handy. As to why a 19-year-old can legally get a gun, the Second Amendment refers to a "well-regulated militia" as necessary for our freedom.

And yes, a 19-year-old is part of the militia.

Section 311 of the U.S. Code Title 10 (as last amended in 1958) says: "(a) The militia of the United States consists of all able-bodied males at least 17 years of age and ... under 45 years of age who are, or who have made a declaration of intention to become, citizens of the United States and of female citizens of the United States who are members of the National Guard."

Third, many on the left want to ban the "mentally ill" from obtaining firearms. Currently firearms cannot be legally possessed by someone determined by a judge to be of danger to himself or to others. What about people who do not meet that standard? It was the left, most prominently the American Civil Liberties Union, that in the 1970s successfully pushed to end "involuntary commitment" for those who do not meet that standard. Bruce Ennis became legal director of the ACLU in 1977 and was known as the father of the "mental health bar." In 1974 he said, "My personal goal is either to abolish involuntary commitment or to set up so many procedural roadblocks and hurdles that it will be difficult, if not impossible, for the state to commit people against their will."

So where does this leave us? Given the large number of defensive uses of guns, that the purpose of the right to keep and bear is to stop government tyranny, and the legal and moral difficulties of taking guns away from "crazy people," Trump's prescription to "harden the target" and eliminate "gun-free zones" makes the most sense.

Tariffs and Economic Populism: Good Politics, Bad Economics

March 8, 2018

We came to expect economic illiteracy from left-wing President Barack Obama.

For example, in attempting to explain away his tepid economic recovery, Obama blamed the emergence of new technologies, which he claimed killed more jobs. "When you go to a bank you use the ATM; you don't go to a bank teller," Obama said. "Or you go to the airport and you use a kiosk instead of checking in at the gate."

As to Obama's claim that ATMs kill teller jobs, Tamar Jacoby of Opportunity America, a pro-growth nonprofit, wrote three years ago: "The number of bank tellers working in the U.S. has risen since the 1970s, when ATMs were introduced. How could that be? The average bank branch used to employ 20 workers. The spread of ATMs reduced the number to about 13, making it cheaper for banks to open branches. Meanwhile, thanks in part to the convenience of the new machines, the number of banking transactions soared, and banks began to compete by promising better customer service: more bank employees, at more branches, handling more complex tasks than tellers in the past."

Again, this is how Democrats think. But what about the faulty economic thinking of conservatives? For example, Fox's usually astute Tucker Carlson recently scolded Amazon for not paying any federal income taxes and for supposedly killing competitors and throwing their workers out of work. "I did (pay federal taxes)," said Carlson, "but also I haven't put tens of thousands of people out of work, like Amazon has. They've hired a lot, but they've put many more out of work. They've destroyed many more businesses than they've created. Look, I get it, that's the nature of market capitalism, but they feel no obligation to give back at all to the federal treasury—at all?"

Is Amazon guilty, as Carlson claims, of destroying "many more businesses than they've created"? Not according to the Foundation for Economic Reform, a free-market think tank. The FEE writes: "As of January (2017), Amazon had 306,800 employees and a promise to hire an additional 100,000 full-time employees by mid-2018. On their own these numbers are impressive, but they do not account for the additional employees who will find future part-time employment via Amazon's participation in the sharing economy." New Federal Reserve Chairman Jerome Powell even credits Amazon with helping to keep inflation low.

What about Carlson's insistence that Amazon possesses an obligation to pay more in taxes than legally required? Learned Hand served as a federal judge from 1909 to 1951. A brilliant thinker and writer, Hand's decisions are studied by law students and frequently cited by other courts. As to a person's obligation to pay taxes, Hand, in one decision, wrote: "Anyone may arrange his affairs so that his taxes shall be as low as possible; he is not bound to choose that pattern which best pays the treasury. There is not even a patriotic duty to increase one's taxes." In another tax case, he wrote: "Over and over again courts have said that there is nothing sinister in so arranging one's affairs as to keep taxes as low as possible. Everybody does so, rich or poor; and all do right, for nobody owes any public duty to pay more than the law demands: taxes are enforced exactions, not voluntary contributions. To demand more in the name of morals is mere cant."

This brings us to President Donald Trump's plan to impose a 25 percent tariff on imported steel and 10 percent on aluminum. We've seen this movie before.

In 2002, President George W. Bush imposed a 30 percent tax on steel imports. The result? The following year, the Heritage Foundation concluded: "Domestically, the steel tariffs ... have hurt more workers than they have helped. That's because industries that use steel to manufacture other products such as auto parts, appliances and buildings produce more products and employ more people than the steel industry does. In fact, according to the Consuming Industries Trade Action Coalition ... for every employee in the steel-producing industry, 59 work in the steel-using industry. The tariffs increased prices in these industries, lowering demand. That's why the Institute for International Economics estimates that as many as 52,000 jobs have been lost in the steel-using industry since the tariffs were enacted." The Peterson Institute for International Economics put the cost of one steel-making industry job saved at $400,000—*per job*.

Economist Milton Friedman, a Reagan friend and unofficial adviser, argued that protectionism discriminates against cheap prices. Friedman, paraphrasing 19th-century economist Henry George, said: "In time of war, we blockade our enemies in order to prevent them from getting goods from us. In time of peace, we do to ourselves by tariffs what we do to our enemy in time of war." Tariffs may be good politics, but they are bad economics.

Obama majored in political science. But Trump has a BS degree in economics from the Wharton School of Finance and Commerce. What's his excuse?

Dem Pundit: 'Paying Off a Porn Star Is Presidential?'

March 15, 2018

When it comes to the issue of porn star Stormy Daniels, we should welcome the media and the Democrats' newfound interest in the treatment—and mistreatment—of women by powerful political figures.

Never mind that whatever relationship Daniels had with President Donald Trump was consensual and ended a decade ago. Nor that there doesn't appear to be any evidence that Trump broke any campaign law regarding the apparent $130K "keep quiet" settlement reached only days before the election. Poor Ms. Daniels—the value of salacious stuff about Trump has skyrocketed now that he is president, so Daniels wants out of the nondisclosure agreement that she willingly signed. She sold cheap, and now wants more.

Even if no laws were broken, the Dems and the media insist that, well, it's the optics. This just looks bad. As one CNN pundit/Democratic strategist put it, "Paying off a porn star is presidential?"

Democrats rate President John F. Kennedy one of the country's best presidents. Kennedy's popularity remains despite the revelations of his reckless and dangerous sexual misbehavior *during* his presidency. The Democratic icon partied with hookers at the White House and bedded a mobster's girlfriend. The Chicago Tribune's Joan Beck, in a column, discussed "The Dark Side of Camelot," a Jack Kennedy expose by former New York Times investigative reporter Seymour Hersh. Beck wrote:

"Many of the charges in 'The Dark Side of Camelot' are now familiar: Joseph Kennedy stole the 1960 election for his son. JFK used the Secret Service to sneak women into the White House when Jackie was away. He botched the invasion of Cuba, leaving brave men to die while he played games of political expediency. He repeatedly tried to have Fidel Castro assassinated. He took huge doses of amphetamines regularly from a feel-good doctor who later lost his license.

"Some of Hersh's accusations are less familiar: Kennedy suffered from venereal disease for 30 years, apparently infecting and being re-infected by the prostitutes and starlets he used to satisfy his insatiable appetite for sex. ... A threat of sexual blackmail had to be defused by giving a $6.5 billion defense contract to General Dynamics. ...

"'In private, Kennedy was consumed with almost daily sexual liaisons and libertine partying, to a degree that shocked many members of his personal Secret Service detail,' writes Hersh. 'The sheer number of Kennedy's sexual partners and the recklessness of his use of them, escalated throughout his presidency.'"

About Bobby Kennedy, his friend Richard Goodwin said it was a "Kennedy family tradition" to philander, but that Bobby was "much more selective and limited" compared to older brother John.

What about another Democrat icon, Ted Kennedy, hailed in death as the Lion of the Senate, even with the long record of his reckless sexual misconduct?

This is from a 1990 GQ article called "Ted Kennedy on the Rocks": "A former mid-level Kennedy staffer, bitterly disillusioned, recalls with disgust one (now ex-) high-ranking aide as 'a pimp ... whose real position was to procure women for Kennedy.' The fellow did have a legitimate job, she says, but also openly bragged of his prowess at getting attractive and beddable dates for his boss."

GQ also detailed one incident in a restaurant's private room: "As (waitress Carla) Gaviglio enters the room, the six-foot-two, 225-plus-pound Kennedy grabs the five-foot-three, 103-pound waitress and throws her on the table. She lands on her back, scattering crystal, plates and cutlery and the lit candles. Several glasses and a crystal candlestick are broken. Kennedy then picks her up from the table and throws her on (drinking buddy Sen. Christopher) Dodd, who is sprawled in a chair. With Gaviglio on Dodd's lap, Kennedy jumps on top and begins rubbing his genital area against hers, supporting his weight on the arms of the chair. As he is doing this, (waitress Betty) Loh enters the room. She and Gaviglio both scream, drawing one or two dishwashers. Startled,

Kennedy leaps up. He laughs. Bruised, shaken and angry over what she considered a sexual assault, Gaviglio runs from the room."

As to President Bill Clinton, the late British left-wing writer Christopher Hitchens, in "No One Left to Lie To," claimed that three women have made "plausible" allegations of rape by Bill Clinton.

Juanita Broaddrick, on "Dateline NBC," claimed that Clinton, then-Arkansas attorney general and gubernatorial candidate, raped her. She further alleges that Hillary Clinton, shortly after the alleged rape, verbally intimidated her, implying that Broaddrick better keep her mouth shut—or else. At a political event two weeks later, Broaddrick claims that Hillary approached her: "She came over to me, took ahold of my hand and said, 'I've heard so much about you and I've been dying to meet you. ... I just want you to know how much that Bill and I appreciate what you do for him.' ... (Hillary Clinton) took ahold of my hand and squeezed it and said, 'Do you understand? *Everything* that you do.'"

To paraphrase, rape is presidential?

No-Drama Obama Versus Trump 'Chaos'

March 22, 2018

Conservative watchdog organization Media Research Center examined the nightly news coverage of President Donald Trump on ABC, NBC and CBS in January and February and concluded that the stories were 91 percent negative. One consistent narrative, particularly given the recent firing of Secretary of State Rex Tillerson, is that "chaos" reigns in the Trump White House.

Never mind that President Barack Obama went through four secretaries of defense and five chiefs of staff. Obama, goes the narrative, calmly navigated the country during his eight-year tenure. Trump, on the other hand, is reckless, dangerous, undisciplined and out of control.

Never mind that the U.S. consumers' confidence is at a level not seen since the early 2000s. Forget the increased value in the stock market, and the appreciation in average home value since the beginning of the Trump presidency. ISIS fighters have been killed or surrendered in the thousands. North Korea's Kim Jong Un has agreed to resume talks about "denuclearization." The Middle East did not set itself on fire when Trump agreed to move the U.S. Embassy from Tel Aviv to Jerusalem. After nearly 14 months, even many Democrats admit they still, after a year of investigations, see no evidence of "collusion" between Russia and the Trump campaign.

But things just look ... chaotic.

President "No-Drama Obama" did indeed successfully push Obamacare through Congress and signed it into law. When the House Democrats first revealed what eventually became Obamacare, the Wall Street Journal called it "the worst bill ever." The Journal wrote: "With spending and debt already at record peacetime levels, the bill creates a new and probably unrepealable middle-class entitlement that is designed to expand over time. Taxes will need to rise precipitously, even as

ObamaCare so dramatically expands government control of health care that eventually all medicine will be rationed via politics." The law did not, as Obama routinely promised, save every family $2,500 a year. Obamacare did not, as the President insisted, "bend the cost curve" down. PolitiFact gave Obama their 2013 "Lie of the Year" award for telling the American people, "If you like your health care plan, you can keep it," a guarantee that Obama made even when he knew it was not true.

As commander in chief, the no-drama President signed the Iran deal that critics argue puts the world's No. 1 sponsor of terror on a path toward getting a nuclear bomb. Obama's first secretary of defense, Robert Gates, said Obama based the deal on a "hope that over a 10-year period with the sanctions being lifted that ... they will abandon their ideology, their theology, their revolutionary principles, their meddling in various parts of the region." Gates called this hope "unrealistic."

Obama, over the objection of his entire national security team, pulled out all the troops from Iraq. Retired Army Gen. Ray Odierno, a member of the Joint Chiefs of Staff, later said he believed ISIS could have been dealt with had we left a stay-behind force.

On the economy, Obama signed a $787 billion so-called stimulus package, averaged $100 billion in new regulations every single year of his presidency, and promoted the silly, wasteful "cash for clunkers" and the equally silly and wasteful "cash for caulkers." Obama defenders argue that the recession Obama dealt with was particularly severe. Yet historically, the deeper the recession, the higher the bounce back. Not so under Obama. The recession President Ronald Reagan dealt with was worse, at least by the metrics the Democrats and the media once used until those very metrics made Democrats look bad.

Unemployment, for example, under Obama reached 10 percent. Under Reagan, it reached 10.8 percent. Inflation was 3.8 percent the year before Obama took office, but dropped to 1.3 percent his last year. Under Reagan, it was 13.5 percent the year before he took office, but dropped to 4.1 his last year. Prime interest rates under Obama, again, were 3.25 percent when he entered office, and remained low at 3.75 when he left. Under Reagan, prime interest rates climbed as high as 20.5 percent and dipped as low as 7.5 percent.

It was a Democrat, Jimmy Carter, who, in running against President Gerald Ford in 1976, use the "misery index." It was simple. Just add up unemployment, plus inflation. The bigger the number, the worse the economy. Carter pointed out that under Ford, the misery index had gone up. Unfortunately for Carter, when he ran for reelection in 1980, Reagan pointed out that the misery index under Carter had grown even larger. Under Obama, at its worst point, the misery index reached 12.97 in 2011. During Reagan's administration, the misery index was at its worst point when he entered office, at 19.33.

Obama, who supposedly governed without drama, delivered the worst recovery since 1949. On the economy and on foreign policy, he signed costly legislation and pushed counterproductive policies. Do Americans want a president who ultimately does the right thing or a president who racks up style points while making one blunder after another?

Where's the Common Sense in 'Common Sense' Gun Laws?

March 29, 2018

Americans, many quite young, attended anti-gun violence rallies across the country. Many protesters demanded more federal "common-sense" gun control laws. But the push for common-sense gun laws lacks common sense, or at least perspective.

The protests, sparked by the murders of 17 people at a high school in Parkland, Florida, were billed as a "March for Our Lives." But according to criminologist James Alan Fox, over the last 25 years 10 students have died each year, on average, in school shootings. By contrast, every year about 300 Americans are struck by lightning. Most survive, but since 2000 an average of 35 people have died each year from lightning strikes.

One "common-sense" proposal is to reenact the "assault weapons" ban.

But of all homicides involving a firearm, only a small percent involve any type of rifle. Furthermore, the assault weapons ban did not achieve the objective of reducing murder and violent crime. Economist John Lott noted: "Since the Federal Assault Weapons Ban expired in September 2004, murder and overall violent-crime rates have fallen. In 2003, the last full year before the law expired, the U.S. murder rate was 5.7 per 100,000 people. ... By 2011, the murder rate fell to 4.7 per 100,000 people. One should also bear in mind that just 2.6 percent of all murders are committed using any type of rifle."

The "common-sense" gun control activists rarely ask, "What about the beneficial effect of gun ownership?" The Centers for Disease Control examined research on the defensive uses of guns. It concluded: "Studies that directly assessed the effect of actual defensive uses of guns (i.e., incidents in which a gun was 'used' by the crime victim in the sense of attacking or threatening an offender) have found consistently lower injury rates among gun-using crime victims compared with victims who used other self-protective strategies."

The CDC's report also found that "defensive use of guns by crime victims is a common occurrence." Exact statistics are hard to find because the police are not always notified, so the number of defensive gun uses is likely understated because they're underreported. "Almost all national survey estimates indicate that defensive gun uses by victims are at least as common as offensive uses by criminals," wrote the CDC, "with estimates of annual uses ranging from about 500,000 to more than 3 million per year, in the context of about 300,000 violent crimes involving firearms in 2008." The CDC noted one study of defensive gun users who believe that but for their own firearm they would have been killed.

Criminologist and researcher Gary Kleck, using his own commissioned phone surveys and number extrapolation, estimates that 2.5 million Americans use guns for defensive purposes each year. One in six of that number, or 400,000, believe someone would have been dead but for their ability to resort to their defensive use of firearms. Kleck points out that if only one-tenth of the people are right about saving a life, the number of people saved annually by guns would still be 40,000.

For some perspective, consider the number of Americans who die each year because of medical errors. A 2016 Johns Hopkins study called medical error the third-leading cause of death in the United States, accounting for about 250,000 deaths annually, or 10 percent of all deaths. Other studies put the number as high as 400,000 a year or more—since medical examiners, morticians and doctors rarely put "human error" or "medical system failure" on a death certificate.

What about accidents that result from driving while texting or engaged in other distracting activities like playing a CD or applying makeup? In 2015, according to the National Highway Traffic Safety Administration, 3,477 people were killed, and 391,000 were injured, in motor vehicle crashes involving distracted drivers.

How many Americans die each year because of opioid abuse? According to the latest estimates from the CDC, more than 50,000 people died from opioid drug overdoses in 2016—15,446 from heroin, 14,427 from prescription opioids and 20,145 from non-methadone synthetic opioids like fentanyl.

Finally, few of the demonstrators, at least publicly, called for the repeal of the Second Amendment. But the former Supreme Court Justice John Paul Stevens calls for the repeal of the Second Amendment on the grounds that it is "a relic of the 18th century." He argues that only a repeal of the Second Amendment would diminish the National Rifle Association's power and influence. Stevens does not even believe that the Founding Fathers intended an "individual right" to keep and bear arms. A repeal would require approval of two-thirds of both Houses of Congress and three-quarters of the states. Good luck with that.

A prediction. When the dust settles and the fury wanes, Congress will not pass additional gun control laws. It won't be for lack of passion. It will because the "common-sense" proposals suggested—banning bump stocks, reenacting the "assault weapons ban" and others—either would do nothing to reduce firearm crime or would violate the Second Amendment. In short, the "common-sense" measures are devoid of common sense.

If Laura Ingraham Goes Down for 'Bullying,' You're Next!

April 5, 2018

What did Fox News' Laura Ingraham say that cost her advertisers?

About David Hogg, the teenage Parkland, Florida, high school shooting survivor, Fox's Ingraham tweeted: "David Hogg Rejected By Four Colleges To Which He Applied and whines about it. (Dinged by UCLA with a 4.1 GPA...totally predictable given acceptance rates.)" Insensitive, given the mass shooting that killed 17 at Hogg's high school? Yes. Insulting and condescending coming from an Ivy League-educated lawyer? Yes. But the punishment does not fit the crime.

Hogg urged Ingraham's advertisers to drop her show. Several did. Ingraham apologized, but Hogg refused to accept her apology. He called her a "bully" and wants Ingraham to extend her apology to others she offended: "She told Lebron James to shut up and dribble. I don't see any apology for those people. ... I would only consider (going back on her show) after she apologizes to all the people that she's hurt throughout her professional career because of her immaturity and unprofessionalism."

Two weeks after the Parkland shooting, Hogg gave an interview to The Outline, in which the writer described Hogg as "exhausted" and "still traumatized." Hogg said:

"What sick f-----s out there want to continue to sell more guns, murder more children, and honestly just get reelected. What type of s----- person does that? They could have blood from children splattered all over their faces and they wouldn't take action, because they all still see these dollar signs."

"When your old-a-- parent is like, 'I don't know how to send an iMessage,' and you're just like, 'Give me the f------ phone and let me handle it.' Sadly, that's what we have to do with our government; our parents don't know how to use a f------ democracy, so we have to."

Referring to Republican Florida Sen. Marco Rubio and money contributed to him by the National Rifle Association, Hogg said: "What about the $176,000 you took for those 17 people's blood?"

But Ingraham is a "bully"?

Now does this "Ingraham Standard" apply to, say, CNN's Anderson Cooper? Frustrated at what he perceived as his guest's blind defense of President Donald Trump, Cooper said, "If (Trump) took a dump on his desk, you would defend him." Cooper apologized, but, then, so did Ingraham.

What about Time Warner's "Real Time With Bill Maher" show on HBO? Here are some of Maher's greatest hits on conservative women:

Sarah Palin is a C-word—an offensive slang word for female genitalia.

Sarah Palin is a "dumb t---," using a derisive slang word for female genitalia.

Sarah Palin's son, who has Down syndrome, is "retarded."

Sarah Palin and Michele Bachmann are "two bimbos."

The Rev. Al Sharpton, an MSNBC host, has an exhaustive list of offensive, incendiary, anti-Semitic comments. At a rally in Harlem in 1991, Sharpton said, "If the Jews want to get it on, tell them to pin their yarmulkes back and come over to my house." A few days later, a 7-year-old black boy was accidentally hit and killed by a car driven by a Jew in the Crown Heights area of Brooklyn, New York. Immediately after the young boy's death, three days of anti-Semitic rioting ensued in Crown Heights, where two people died and almost 200 were wounded. Surrounded by a mob yelling, "Kill the Jew!" a young Talmudic scholar was stabbed to death. Many believe Sharpton's rhetoric played a role in fomenting the Crown Heights riots. A Columbia University professor called it "a modern-day pogrom."

At the 7-year-old boy's funeral Sharpton said: "The world will tell us he was killed by accident. Yes, it was a social accident. ... It's an accident to allow an apartheid ambulance service in the middle of Crown Heights. ... Talk about how Oppenheimer in South Africa sends diamonds straight to Tel Aviv and deals with the diamond merchants right here in Crown Heights. The issue is not anti-Semitism; the issue is apartheid. ... All we want to say is what Jesus said: If you offend one of these little ones, you got to pay for it. No compromise, no meetings, no kaffeeklatsch, no skinnin' and grinnin'. Pay for your deeds."

What about CNN's Don Lemon, who called President Trump "racist" following reports that Trump called Haiti and African counties "s---hole countries"? When Fox's then-host Glenn Beck call Obama "racist" a group called Color Of Change put up an online petition calling for the cancellation of Beck's show.

If Ingraham is a "bully," what do you call MSNBC's caustic, Trump-hating lineup of hosts? Apply the Ingraham Standard to MSNBC's Chris Matthews. Angry with the Republican opposition to Obamacare, Matthews tore into the GOP and accused the Party of wanting "people who don't have insurance to die on the gurney."

As for Hogg, especially when complaining about "parents," he sounds like a teenager. Oh, wait, he is.

Why Is Facebook Groveling?

April 12, 2018

What is it about spectacular American business success stories like Facebook that brings out envy and resentment? Facebook has 2 billion monthly users. CEO Mark Zuckerberg is 33 and has a net worth north of $60 billion, making him the fifth richest person on Earth, according to Forbes last month. His company is also accused of allowing "misuse" of its users' personal data to help elect President Donald Trump. Never mind that the 2012 Obama campaign bragged about using Facebook in a similar way to win re-election. So, when it comes to Facebook and Zuckerberg, what's not to hate?

Industrial pioneers and visionaries like John D. Rockefeller in oil and Andrew Carnegie in steel found themselves vilified in newspapers as "robber barons," a label popularized by a New York Times writer. Never mind that the price for kerosene continued to fall even as Rockefeller dominated the industry, just as the price of steel continued to fall despite Carnegie's alleged greed.

IBM found itself under investigation by the Department of Justice in 1969 for antitrust violations. Those complaining about the company's alleged abuses were not consumers but competitors. IBM management devoted so much time and resources to fighting the antitrust lawsuit until it was dropped 13 years later for being "without merit" that business suffered. One could argue that IBM never fully recovered.

Microsoft became a target of antitrust regulators at the DOJ in 2001 for the company's alleged illegal "bundling." Then-CEO Bill Gates learned that without lobbying clout in Washington D.C., the regulators could come knocking. And they did.

Now comes Facebook. Full disclosure: I do not have a personal Facebook page. I never understood why people willingly give out information on their personal lives, whether there are in a relationship, etc., on a billboard for anybody to see. Clearly, 2 billion Facebook users disagree with me.

Perhaps what aggravates people is founder Zuckerberg's shifting statements about the use of collected personal data, and his blather about wanting Facebook to connect the whole world in order to "do good." Guess he thinks nobody saw the movie "The Social Network" and the vicious big-money lawsuit he was involved in over who founded Facebook. Zuckerberg is a businessman.

Zuckerberg agreed to testify before Congress to address accusations of "violating the privacy" of users' personal data. What privacy? The agreement between Facebook and users could not be more clear: Facebook can collect your data. Facebook can and will use your personal data to make money. Its privacy policy states in part:

"Depending on which Services you use, we collect different kinds of information from or about you.

"Things you do and information you provide. We collect the content and other information you provide when you use our Services, including when you sign up for an account, create or share, and message or communicate with others. This can include information in or about the content you provide, such as the location of a photo or the date a file was created. We also collect information about how you use our Services, such as the types of content you view or engage with or the frequency and duration of your activities.

"Things others do and information they provide. We also collect content and information that other people provide when they use our Services, including information about you, such as when they share a photo of you, send a message to you, or upload, sync or import your contact information.

"Your networks and connections. We collect information about the people and groups you are connected to and how you interact with them, such as the people you communicate with the most or the groups you like to share with. We also collect contact information you provide if you upload, sync or import this information (such as an address book) from a device. ...

"Information from websites and apps that use our Services. We collect information when you visit or use third-party websites and apps that use our Services (like when they offer our Like button or Facebook

Log In or use our measurement and advertising services). This includes information about the websites and apps you visit, your use of our Services on those websites and apps, as well as information the developer or publisher of the app or website provides to you or us."

Facebook's business model is to collect personal data so that advertisers can precisely target prospective customers, an extremely lucrative enterprise. A 2013 book called "Unauthorized Access" put it this way: "The ability to create detailed psychographic profiles makes Facebook a potential targeted advertising gold mine. ... But Facebook doesn't need to—or want to—*transfer to third parties* any of its valuable data on its users. Instead, advertisers specify their desired targets to Facebook, and Facebook uses the profiles to match advertising to the specification."

Would this public flogging of Zuckerberg have occurred had Hillary Clinton won the election? And many Republicans, who should know better, joined in the Facebook condemnation. There is no such thing as a free lunch. If you think something is free, you are likely the commodity.

Comey Tells Ex-Clinton Aide Stephanopoulos That Trump Is 'Morally Unfit'

April 19, 2018

Fired ex-FBI head James Comey told ABC News "chief anchor" George Stephanopoulos that Donald Trump is "morally unfit to be president"? Think about this. Comey offered this assessment to *Stephanopoulos*, whose former boss, first candidate and then President Bill Clinton, was credibly accused of rape and sexual assault, had sex in the Oval Office with an intern, and then lied about it under oath, for which he was impeached.

But Comey tells Stephanopoulos that Trump is "morally unfit to be president"?

Also, Fox News' Sean Hannity, a staunch President Trump defender, got hammered for not revealing his relationship with Donald Trump's attorney, Michael Cohen. Hannity claims his relationship with Cohen did not rise to client-attorney, but that he had merely sought out Cohen's informal advice on real estate matters. Still, Hannity, now the face of Fox News, who at times has referred to himself as a "journalist," should have known that critics would cry "conflict of interest." So he should have disclosed the relationship out of abundance of caution.

Shouldn't "chief anchor" Clintonopoulos have also given *full disclosure?* Shouldn't he have informed the viewers that he was a top campaign aide for then-Gov. Clinton's presidential race; that he helped Hillary Clinton malign Bill's female accusers; and that after the election he served as a top aide to President Clinton?

Why didn't Stephanopoulos disclose that as a top campaign aide to Bill Clinton, he went on TV and accused Gennifer Flowers, a Clinton mistress, of lying? And yet with Comey, Stephanopoulos clenches his jaw in indignation over Trump's alleged treatment of women.

Stephanopoulos, in his Comey interview, never challenged the ex-FBI director's assertion that Trump is "morally unfit" to be president. Democratic icon President John F. Kennedy, according to former New York Times reporter and New Yorker contributor Seymour Hersh, had venereal disease for decades, slept with a mobster's mistress, partied with hookers in the White House, etc. But Trump's "morally unfit"?! Stephanopoulos *never* asked Comey how and why he found that Hillary Clinton lacked "intent" to violate the Espionage Act—when the provision in question *does not require intent*. All it requires is "gross negligence."

If the goal of Comey's book was to defend his reputation, it's not working. Former New York Times statistician and writer Nate Silver tweeted: "It's also not particularly honorable, if you have information that you believe is of immediate and vital national importance, to wait to 11 months to release it until you can have a giant book launch and publicity tour around it."

If anti-Trumpers were hoping for a smoking gun, Comey didn't not deliver. First, he flat-out admits that politics colored his decision to re-open the Hillary Clinton email investigation days before the election. He writes: "It is entirely possible that, because I was making decisions in an environment where Hillary Clinton was sure to be the next president, my concern about making her an illegitimate president by concealing the restarted investigation bore greater weight than it would have if the election appeared closer or if Donald Trump were ahead in all polls."

Second, Comey says he doesn't know if Trump broke the law. "I have one perspective on the behavior I saw," Comey writes, "which while disturbing and violating basic norms of ethical leadership, may fall short of being illegal."

Meanwhile, the Trump-Russia collusion investigation continues without, so far, evidence of Trump-Russia collusion, while the media's Trump Derangement Syndrome rages on. Anti-Republicanism has, of course, long been a staple of the mainstream political news media. In the 40-plus years The Washington Post has been endorsing presidential candidates, they have never endorsed a Republican. The New York Times has not endorsed a Republican president in 60 years—since Dwight D. Eisenhower in 1956. But this is a whole new level of hostility.

America would be on fire had President Barack Obama spent the first year and a half of his presidency battling bogus charges of Russian "collusion," and then an Obama collusion probe turned into an investigation about lying to investigators; expanded into an investigation of obstruction of justice; became an investigation of tax fraud; and morphed into an investigation about the validity of a nondisclosure agreement with a porn star with whom the President may or may not have had a sexual relationship with 12 years ago.

Even Democratic former President Jimmy Carter, a few months ago, offered this observation about Trump and his treatment by the media: "I think the media have been harder on Trump than any other president certainly that I've known about. I think they feel free to claim that Trump is mentally deranged and everything else without hesitation."

Comey is making millions, but his reputation is now in tatters. As for the hard leftists at MSNBC who accuse Hannity of violating journalistic standards, there is but a two-word response: Al Sharpton.

Joe Biden, Dems and the Race Card: They Don't Leave Home Without It

April 26, 2018

Former Vice President Joe Biden recently told MSNBC's Rev. Al Sharpton that the GOP wants voter identification laws for one reason. Racist Republicans so despise blacks and are so determined to oppress them, that they seek to prevent all blacks from voting.

Biden said: "It's what these guys are all about, man. These Republicans don't want working-class people voting. They don't want black folks voting." What Republicans "are all about," according to Biden, is the push in some states for voter ID laws, which Democrats call "voter suppression." Then-Attorney General Eric Holder characterized the call for voter ID laws as an example of "pernicious" racism.

If it is "pernicious" racism, apparently a lot of people failed to get the memo. Blacks want voter ID laws, too. A 2016 Gallup Poll found: "Though many of the arguments for early voting and against voter ID laws frequently cite minorities' voting access, nonwhites' views of the two policies don't differ markedly from those of whites. Seventy-seven percent of nonwhites favor both policies, while whites favor each at 81 percent." This has not stopped the Democrats from turning the legitimate concern about the integrity of voting into a full-on attack against blacks.

Biden, of course, is a skilled veteran at playing the race card. Recall how then-Vice President Biden, in 2012, somehow turned then-GOP presidential candidate Mitt Romney's opposition to the 2010 Dodd-Frank financial reform bill into a racial issue. "(Romney) is going to let the big banks once again write their own rules, unchain Wall Street,"

Biden said at a campaign event in Danville, Virginia. "He is going to put y'all back in chains."

Without the 90-plus percent black vote, the Democratic Party, at the national level, is in deep trouble. This explains why they race-bait. Constantly.

Take then-senate candidate Claire McCaskill, D-Mo., who, after Hurricane Katrina, said, "(President) George (W.) Bush let people die on rooftops in New Orleans because they were poor and because they were black."

Hillary Clinton, during the 2016 campaign, complained about what she called the "school-to-prison pipeline." Clinton said: "We've seen a significant increase in police involvement in school discipline, especially in schools with majority-black students. We're seeing an overreliance on suspensions and expulsions. I'm sure many of us remember that horrifying video of the girl in South Carolina being thrown out of her desk and dragged across her classroom by a school police officer. A classroom should be a safe place for our children. We shouldn't even have to say that, I don't think. So today I'm announcing my plan to end the school-to-prison pipeline." So the cops lie in wait to arrest innocent young blacks? Not one word about personal responsibility?

Actor Denzel Washington, whose last movie was about a criminal defense lawyer, commented on a criminal justice system that many call institutionally racist, resulting in an unfair mass incarceration of blacks. But Washington wasn't buying it. He said: "It starts in the home. You know, if the father is not in the home, the boy will find a father in the streets. I saw it in my generation and in every generation before me, and in every one since. ... If the streets raise you, then the judge becomes your mother, and, you know, prison becomes your home." As a result, Washington said, "So, you know, I can't blame the system." In other words, the breakdown or, more precisely, the nonformation of the nuclear black family is a far, far bigger problem than the allegedly racist criminal justice system.

But as long as the Democratic Party continues to market itself as the party of social justice in an ever-racist America, the party thinks it can capture the black vote. Who cares whether it's counterproductive for Dems to tell young blacks that hard work doesn't pay off? It's the votes that matter. Former Washington Post investigative journalist Ron Kessler wrote in his book, "Inside The White House," that President Lyndon Johnson, in touting the Civil Rights Act of 1964, said, "I'll have those (N-words) voting Democratic for the next 200 years."

President Donald Trump, through his secretary of education, urges parental choice in schools. Polls show that inner-city parents want the option to remove their kid from underperforming public schools, where many of those who graduate cannot read or do math at grade level. Many graduate without the skills employers want. Many of those pursuing higher education must take remedial courses to compete at the college level. Yet to Biden and the Democrats, Trump, who wants to do something about the quality of education in inner cities, is "racist." And "racist" Trump wants to eliminate the competition for jobs held by illegal aliens. Research by Harvard economist George Borjas shows that illegals, especially unskilled illegals, compete for inner-city jobs and place downward pressure on wages. The Americans losing out are the very black and brown workers the Democratic Party claims they care so deeply about.

But that doesn't stop the Democrats from employing their tried-and-true technique. The race card. Don't leave home without it.

Trump's 2 Big Advantages: Time and Low Expectations

May 3, 2018

Despite the daily pounding he receives from the media, President Donald Trump enjoys two advantages—low expectations and lots of time.

When the opposition party and their media cohorts call Trump an idiot, a fool, a liar, racist, sexist, homophobic, anti-immigrant, anti-Mexican, incompetent, lazy, unfocused, greedy, hateful, fascist, tyrannical and/or Hitler-esque, there's really nowhere to go but up. Recall how immediately after Trump took office, "experts" predicted a short administration, perhaps of months-long duration. Critics said Trump did not really think he would win. The recent anti-Trump book by Michael Wolff even claims that Trump *did not want* to win. Some even predicted that Trump, having captured the presidency, would grow bored and quickly return to his construction business.

This brings us to Trump's second advantage, time. There is a long time between now and November, let alone between now and the end of Trump's second term. The piling-on in the first year and a half of the Trump presidency contradicts a reality, quite annoying to Trump bashers: The man is fulfilling one campaign promise after another.

The Obama administration, for example, complained about our NATO partners' failure to spend the expected amount on national security. After Trump loudly complained that only five of the 29 member nations spend the minimum NATO requirement of 2 percent of their gross domestic product on defense; that America was being used and financially ripped off by an "obsolete" NATO, which doesn't fight terrorism; and that member nations need to "promptly pay their bills," what happened? Several members pledged to increase their military spending.

How many Republican presidential candidates over the years complained about the ban on drilling for oil in Alaska's Arctic National Wildlife Refuge, known as ANWR? Trump signed legislation to begin the process of repealing the ban. Trump successfully appointed more federal appellate judges than any first-year president in history. Trump lowered the corporate tax rate, once the highest statutory rate in the industrialized world. Trump, as promised, eliminated or delayed numerous job-killing regulations. He approved the construction of the Keystone XL and Dakota Access pipelines.

The stock market has repeatedly reached all-time highs, and for the first time in years, polls show that Americans believe young peoples' lives will be better than their parents'. An April 2018 Gallup poll found 61 percent believe today's youth "will have a better life than their parents did," the highest mark since 2010.

When Trump derisively called North Korean dictator Kim Jong Un "rocket man," critics practically counted down our remaining days on earth before we would see mushroom clouds. As the only President ever with neither political nor military experience, Trump was called everything from a warmonger to naive. In January, former Vice President Joe Biden said, "(North Korea) is not a game. This is not about 'can I puff my chest out bigger than yours.' (Trump's threat) is just not—it's not presidential."

President Trump, shortly after taking office, placed American aircraft carriers in the Sea of Japan. Three aircraft carriers and their multi-ship strike groups conducted war exercises in mid-November. Well, well. It was not long after this that Kim Jong Un became the first North Korean dictator to set foot on South Korean soil. Kim announced plans to end the 68-year-old Korean War and even promised to "denuclearize," as Trump demanded as a condition of removing economic sanctions.

Ronald Reagan would caution the new President to "trust, but verify," and there's a long way to go before Trump can declare victory on the North Korean issue. But even Trump haters, whether or not they give Trump credit, must admit that the world is better off with a North Korea without nuclear weapons.

Trump's achievements are all the more impressive given that from the beginning of his presidency he has been under investigation for allegedly "colluding" with the Russians to win the election. The collusion investigation has apparently evolved into an investigation of lying to investigators, obstruction of justice, money laundering and possible campaign finance violation over the $130K payoff to porn star Stormy Daniels.

There is an irony here. Many of the Trump bashers cheering special counsel Robert Mueller's probe also called the impeachment of President Bill Clinton a "witch hunt." To this day, many believe Congress impeached Clinton because of his extramarital affair in the White House with an intern. In fact, the House impeached him because he lied under oath and committed obstruction of justice. He was later found in contempt of court for lying and temporarily lost his license to practice law. Former California Republican Congressman James Rogan was a House manager, one of the House members who agreed to prosecute Clinton in the Senate. Rogan, now a judge, said that had Congress done nothing to Clinton it would have set a precedent that a president can, without consequences, lie under oath. And if a president can lie under oath, argued Rogan, why can't any person justify or rationalize lying under oath?

Had Clinton not been impeached, and had the precedent been established that presidents could lie under oath, Trump would have little to fear from a "perjury trap."

Democrats' War on Capitalism

May 10, 2018

Hillary Clinton recently offered yet another reason why she lost her second consecutive race for the presidency: capitalism.

At the Shared Value Leadership Summit in New York City, Clinton was asked whether her self-proclaimed "capitalist" stance hurt her during the 2016 presidential primary season. "It's hard to know," she said, "but I mean, if you're in the Iowa caucuses and 41 percent of Democrats are socialists or self-described socialists, and I'm asked, 'Are you a capitalist?' and I say, 'Yes, but with appropriate regulation and appropriate accountability.' You know, that probably gets lost in the 'Oh, my gosh, she's a capitalist!'"

Clinton's right. Being a Democrat and a "capitalist" is an increasingly untenable position for a politician. Polls show that today's Democratic Party and capitalism appear to be on a collision course. A November 2015 New York Times/CBS News poll found that 56 percent of Democratic primary voters said they held a positive view of socialism. A Morning Consult/Politico survey in June 2017 asked if a hypothetical replacement for House Minority Leader Nancy Pelosi should be a socialist or capitalist. More Democrats opted for socialism, with 35 percent saying it's somewhat or very important that her replacement be a socialist, while only 31 percent said the same for a capitalist.

Indeed, one of the Democrats' loudest voices, filmmaker Michael Moore, recently praised Karl Marx, the ideological godfather of communism. Moore tweeted: "Happy 200th Birthday Karl Marx! You believed that everyone should have a seat at the table & that the greed of the rich would eventually bring us all down. You believed that everyone deserves a slice of the pie. You knew that the super wealthy were out to grab whatever they could. ... Though the rich have sought to distort him or even use him, time has shown that, in the end, Marx was actually mostly right & that the aristocrats, the slave owners, the bankers and Goldman Sachs were wrong... 'Happy Birthday, Karl Marx. You Were Right!'" Tell that to the millions who died under communist repression in, among other places, China, the Soviet Union and Cambodia.

Perhaps no issue reflects this socialist view more than the Democrats' push for "single-payer" health care. As a state senator, Barack Obama said: "I happen to be a proponent of a single-payer, universal health care program. I see no reason why the United States of America, the wealthiest country in the history of the world, spending 14 percent of its gross national product on health care, cannot provide basic health insurance to everybody. ... A single-payer health care plan, a universal health care plan. That's what I'd like to see. But as all of you know, we may not get there immediately." A few years later, then-presidential candidate Obama reiterated his stance, that if "starting from scratch" he'd have a single-payer system.

Former Democratic National Committee Chairman Howard Dean called the so-called "public option" the end game: "I think while someday we may end up with a single-payer system, it's clear that we're not going to do it all at once, so I think both candidates' (Hillary Clinton's and Obama's) health care plans are a big step forward."

Former Senate Democratic Majority Leader Harry Reid also said that he, too, wants to get to "single-payer." The Las Vegas Sun reported in 2013: "In just about seven weeks, people will be able to start buying Obamacare-approved insurance plans through the new health care exchanges. But already, Senate Majority Leader Harry Reid is predicting those plans," wrote the Sun, "and the whole system of distributing them, will eventually be moot. ... 'What we've done with Obamacare is have a step in the right direction, but we're far from having something that's going to work forever,' Reid said. When then asked by panelist Steve Sebelius whether he meant ultimately the country would have to have a health care system that abandoned insurance as the means of accessing it, Reid said: 'Yes, yes. Absolutely, yes.'"

The "you didn't build that" left does not recognize the relationship between prosperity and allowing people to keep what they produce to the fullest degree possible. By the end of eight years under President Obama, according to the conservative Heritage Foundation, we had less "economic freedom." The United States' score on "economic freedom"—which looks at taxes and regulations, among other criteria—dropped to its lowest level in the 23 years since Heritage began publishing its annual rankings of 180 countries. It is no coincidence that this loss of economic freedom under Obama helped produce the worst American economic recovery since 1949.

Last week brought more good news for Democrats. A Rasmussen poll found that nearly half of American likely voters support a guaranteed government job for all. This is likely to become a central presidential campaign issue for Democrats in 2020. Democrats believe that there is a free lunch and that capitalists are stopping them from eating it.

Fake Russian Ads Stoked Racial Tensions—Race-Hustling Democrats 'Colluded'

May 17, 2018

President Donald Trump rejects the narrative that Russia wanted him to win. USA Today examined each of the 3,517 Facebook ads bought by the Russian-based Internet Research Agency, the company that employed 12 of the 13 Russians indicted by special counsel Robert Mueller for interfering with the 2016 election. It turns out only about 100 of its ads explicitly endorsed Trump or opposed Hillary Clinton.

Most of the fake ads focused on racial division, with many of the ads attempting to exploit what Russia perceives, or wants America to perceive, as severe racial tension between blacks and whites.

Think of it. Vladimir Putin, president of a formerly communist country with the blood of possibly tens of millions of its own people on its hands, is using the race card in America, the least-racist majority-white country in the world, a country that just a few years ago elected and reelected a black person for president. Putin therefore "colludes" with race-card carrying Democrats like Rep. Maxine Waters, D-Calif., who once called the "good" Bush, George Herbert Walker Bush, a "racist." Then there's former Vice President Joe Biden, who recently told the Rev. Al "no justice, no peace" Sharpton: "It's what these guys are all about, man. These Republicans don't want working-class people voting. They don't want black folks voting."

Sharpton, earlier this year, said that Trump "is someone who's chosen a path that is absolutely racism with steroids." Sharpton also wrote: "There were hopes last year that the executive office would temper some of this pettiness, but sadly we now see this is not the case. Rather than attempt to grow and learn, Trump has leaned into his role as divider-in-chief. This is exactly the same racially divisive, unapologetic blowhard I knew in New York."

Sharpton lectures Republicans on political etiquette?

Is this the same Sharpton who shot to fame by falsely accusing a white man of raping a black woman? Is this the same Sharpton, who, according to The New York Times in 2014, owes "more than $4.5 million in current state and federal tax"? Is this the same Sharpton who called the black then-mayor of New York City, David Dinkins, a "n---whore"?

CNN's Don Lemon recently said: "Critical thinking is important as a journalist. If you cannot surmise that this President—if he's not racist, he's certainly racist-adjacent. ... We have come to a consensus in our society that facts matter. ... I feel like it's my obligation as a journalist to say it."

Aside from routinely being called "racist," President Trump is denounced on left-wing cable shows and late-night television as a "liar." MSNBC's Lawrence O'Donnell, a former aide to Sen. Daniel Patrick Moynihan, D-N.Y., called Trump "a pathological liar." CNN's Don Lemon opened a recent show by discussing "the 3,000 lies that the President has told since inauguration."

Trump's "lies" pale in comparison with the Big Lies of the modern left.

The left insists, teaches, preaches and indoctrinates that racism remains a major problem in America. So-called "civil rights" organizations—like Black Lives Matter, the NAACP or the Southern Poverty Law Center—denounce alleged "institutional" or "systemic" or "structural" racism as a serious problem in America, even as racism continues to recede.

The left insists that "sexism" remains a major problem in America. Women, President Barack Obama insisted, earn only 77 cents on the dollar compared with men while performing the same work. Even Obama's Department of Labor called it untrue. In 2009, the Labor Department found that, after controlling for obvious education and job differences, the gender "wage gap" shrank to only 95 percent. The Labor Department found that women often make different choices than men: "A greater percentage of women than men tend to work part-time. Part-time work tends to pay less than full-time work. A greater percentage of women than men tend to leave the labor force for childbirth, child care and elder care. ...

"Research also suggests that differences not incorporated into the model due to data limitations may account for part of the remaining gap. ... Much of the literature, including the Bureau of Labor Statistics ... focus on wages rather than total compensation. Research indicates that women may value non-wage benefits more than men do, and as a result prefer to take a greater portion of their compensation in the form of health insurance and other fringe benefits."

The left insists that the rich are getting richer, while the poor are getting poorer. Actually, the percentage of the world living in "extreme poverty"—currently less than $1.90 a day—has plummeted in the last three decades. In 1990, the United Nations set a goal to cut the world's poverty rate in half by 2015. That goal was reached five years early: By 2010, over a billion people had escaped extreme poverty in just 20 years.

Thanks to a media obsessed with racism, sexism and inequality, and Democrats who play the race card for votes, the Russians have willing accomplices in spreading dissent. After all, President Barack Obama claimed that racism is part of America's "DNA."

Somewhere, Putin is smiling. Yet none dare call it "collusion."

In Calling MS-13 Gang Members 'Animals,' Trump Was Kind

May 24, 2018

President Donald Trump doubled down on calling members of a notorious street gang "animals." Good for him for not backing down and for shining a light on an outrageous phenomenon, especially in Southern California: Latino gangs that target blacks, whether or not they belong to gangs, for death.

Trump, during a roundtable discussion last week with state and local officials from California about so-called sanctuary laws, said: "Deadly and unconstitutional sanctuary state laws ... (offer) safe harbor to some of the most vicious and violent offenders on earth, like MS-13 gang members, putting innocent men, women and children at the mercy of these sadistic criminals."

Margaret Mims, the sheriff of Northern California's Fresno County, talked about the problems caused by the state's so-called sanctuary laws, and that such laws made it harder "to find the bad guys." Mims said, "There could be an MS-13 gang member I know about: If they don't reach a certain threshold (under California's sanctuary laws) I cannot tell ICE (Immigration and Customs Enforcement) about it."

That's when Trump dropped the "A-word."

In response to Sheriff Mims' comments, Trump said: "We have people coming into the country—or trying to come in; we're stopping a lot of them. But we're taking people out of the country. You wouldn't believe how bad these people are. These aren't people. These are animals. And we're taking them out of the country at a level and at a rate that's never happened before."

Sen. Chuck Schumer, D-N.Y., immediately pounced. The Senate minority leader tweeted: "When all of our great-great-grandparents came to America they weren't 'animals,' and these people aren't either."

But even NBC's Chuck Todd admitted that his media colleagues widely misrepresented the President's remarks, especially the initial media reports that failed to note that Trump was referring to MS-13. "This is where I think that my colleagues do us all harm," Todd said. "You know, cover this legitimately. There is plenty of legitimate stuff to ding him on, if you think he deserves to be dinged on. Just be careful. Don't be sloppy about it." As for the "A-word," Todd said: "A lot of people have called violent anybody animals. Anybody who is a violent criminal, in my book, can get called an animal if they're sitting there mauling, killing and raping people. I don't care where they're from."

Cue the selective outrage. Where was this concern for civility when Hillary "deplorables" Clinton said the NRA reminded her of the "Iranians" and the "communists"? Recall, too, Clinton's own "animals"-type description of some black criminals. In 1996, Clinton said: "We need to take these people on. They are often connected to big drug cartels. They are not just gangs of kids anymore. They are often the kinds of kids that are called superpredators."

Calling the MS-13 gang members "animals" is positively mild compared with what the liberal Southern Poverty Law Center said about other vicious Latino gangs. In 2007, the SPLC published a report called: "Latino Gang Members in Southern California Are Terrorizing and Killing Blacks."

Some highlights:

"While the vast majority of hate crimes nationwide are not committed by members of organized groups, Los Angeles County is a different story. Researchers found that in areas with high concentrations, or 'clusters,' of hate crimes, the perpetrators were typically members of Latino street gangs who were purposely targeting blacks. ...

"Mexican Mafia leaders, or shot callers ... have issued a "green light" on all blacks. A sort of gang-life fatwah, this amounts to a standing authorization for Latino gang members to prove their mettle by terrorizing or even murdering any blacks sighted in a neighborhood claimed by a gang loyal to the Mexican Mafia. ...

"Anti-black violence conducted by Latino gangs in Los Angeles has been ongoing for more than a decade. A 1995 Los Angeles Police Department (LAPD) report about Latino gang activity in the Normandale Park neighborhood declared, 'This gang has been involved in an ongoing program to eradicate black citizens from the gang neighborhood.' A 1996 LAPD report on gangs in east Los Angeles stated, 'Local gangs will attack any black person that comes into the city.' ...

"The LAPD estimates there are now 22,000 Latino gang members in the city of Los Angeles alone. That's not only more than all the Crips and the Bloods; it's more than all black, Asian, and white gang members combined. Almost all of those Latino gang members in L.A.—let alone those in other California cities—are loyal to the Mexican Mafia. Most have been thoroughly indoctrinated with the Mexican Mafia's violent racism during stints in prison, where most gangs are racially based. ...

"'It's almost anywhere in L.A. that you could find yourself in a difficult position (as a black person),' says (a) LAPD probation officer. 'All blacks are on green light no matter where.'"

Trump, in calling brutal gang members "animals," did not go far enough.

Roseanne Is Out? Explain Maher, Sharpton and Olbermann

May 31, 2018

Roseanne Barr lost her new television show.

Barr, in a tweet about Barack Obama aide Valerie Jarrett, said of Jarrett: "muslim brotherhood & planet of the apes had a baby=vj." The comedian deleted the offensive tweet, but the damage was irreversible. The reaction was swift.

The Rev. Al Sharpton tweeted: "The comparison ... of ... Valerie Jarrett to an APE is racist and inexcusable. ABC must take action NOW!" The Disney-owned ABC issued the following statement: "Roseanne's Twitter statement is abhorrent, repugnant and inconsistent with our values, and we have decided to cancel her show." Barr left Disney little choice. Standing by her would have meant advertiser boycotts, forcing any company that advertises on her show to explain their association with a "racist."

But what are the rules?

Disney also owns ESPN, the sports cable channel that employs Keith Olbermann, whose angry, unhinged tweets about President Donald Trump make Barr's anti-Jarrett tweet look like a love note. Here's one Olbermann tweeted at Ivanka Trump, Trump's daughter: "Then tell your racist, white supremacist, neo-nazi father to get the f--- out of our society." One would think that Disney would find Olbermann's tweets "abhorrent, repugnant and inconsistent with (their) values."

As for MSNBC's Sharpton, he also said that Barr's tweet shows that Trump is "normalizing" racism. Remember Sharpton became famous by falsely accusing a white man of raping a black teen. A New York grand jury called the accusation a hoax, and Sharpton was successfully sued for defamation. But to this day, Sharpton refuses to apologize. Sharpton helped fan the flames during the deadly 1991 Crown Heights, New York, riots by leading some 400 protesters through the predominately Jewish section of Brooklyn. Days before the deadly riots, Sharpton said at a rally in Harlem, "If the Jews want to get it on, tell them to pin their yarmulkes back and come over to my house." Sharpton once called David Dinkins, the first and only black New York City mayor, a "n----- whore." Sharpton described Jews as "diamond merchants" and whites moving into Harlem as "interlopers." Unwilling to wait for the Ferguson grand jury to finish its investigation of the police shooting death of Michael Brown, Sharpton took to the streets of Ferguson yelling, "No justice, no peace." The grand jury exonerated the officer. No remorse by Sharpton. No apology. No cancellation of his show.

Bill Maher has long hosted a show on HBO and gets top pundits to appear. No guest seems bothered by Maher's sexist, vicious put-downs of Republican women. In his stand-up, Maher called Sarah Palin a "c---" and a "dumb t---"—both offensive and derisive slang words for female genitalia. Maher defended himself by insisting that in his stand-up act, political correctness is off-limits. Michael Richards committed career suicide when, during a comedy stand-up, he shouted down black hecklers by repeatedly using the N-word. That this occurred in a stand-up act was no defense for him. Richards has barely been heard from since.

Maher also called Palin and Michele Bachmann "two bimbos." Maher referred to Palin's son with Down syndrome as "retarded." In January 2013, Maher said that Donald Trump should prove he wasn't "the spawn of his mother having sex with an orangutan." Isn't this pretty much what Barr said?

Meanwhile at CNN, Erin Burnett hosts a daily show. When Burnett worked for MSNBC, she referred to then-President George Bush, standing in a group of politicians, as "the monkey in the middle." CNN's Van Jones called Trump's election a "whitelash," and fellow host Don Lemon, who calls himself a "journalist," recently pronounced President Trump "a racist." Well, that settles that.

One can't even keep track of the many offensive things said on the Disney-owned ABC show "The View." Panelist Sunny Hostin attributed Trump's victory to racism: "Twenty percent of people voted because of racism, and I think after eight years of a black president there was no way that (Clinton) was going to win."

The outrage over Barr's offensive tweet is understandable. But why is there a no-fly zone over Maher, Olbermann and Sharpton? Laura Ingraham took a relatively mild swipe at Parkland gun control activist David Hogg, apologized, but had to weather an advertiser boycott.

The swift cancellation of Barr's show demonstrates yet again that the National Review editor John O'Sullivan was right. "White racism," Sullivan said, "does exist, but its social power is weak and the social power arrayed against it is overwhelming."

Black Motorists Lying on Cops—Who's Doing the 'Racial Profiling'?

June 7, 2018

In the last few weeks, *three* black motorists, including an NAACP chapter president, made blatantly false allegations against perfectly courteous police officers.

Now who's "racially profiling"?

First, in Timmonsville, S.C., local NAACP President the Rev. Jerrod Moultrie put up a lengthy post on his Facebook page: "Tonight, I was racially profiled by Timmonsville Officer CAUSE I WAS DRIVING A MERCEDES BENZ AND GOING HOME IN A NICE NEIGHBORHOOD." The reverend claimed the officer told him, "I am doing you a favor tonight not taking you to jail or writing you a ticket."

Timmonsville Police Chief Billy Brown said Moultrie contacted him the next morning with his accusations of racial profiling and mistreatment. "He made a comment that the officer accused him of having drugs in the car," said Brown. "He said that his wife and grandchild was in the car. He asked them not to move because the officer looked as if he might shoot them or something. He also made mention that the officer continued to ask him about his neighborhood. Why was he in that neighborhood? And (threatened) to put him in jail in reference to something dealing with the registration to the vehicle."

But Chief Brown reviewed the body cam video of the four-minute traffic stop. It showed a very polite officer explaining he pulled the car over for failing to signal a left turn and reminding the occupants to wear their seat belts. Brown said: "When I saw the video, I was shocked that someone who is supposed to be a community leader, a pastor, and head of the NAACP would just come out and tell a blatant lie. It bothered me. It really bothered me, thinking about the racial unrest it could've cost in the community and it's just troubling to me that someone who held a position like that would come out and just tell a lie." The Rev. Moultrie removed his original Facebook post, and refused further comment.

Second, a black South Carolina woman said she had a "traumatic experience" in Virginia when pulled over for speeding and "threatened" by a "white cop." Dawn Hilton-Williams posted an 11-minute Facebook Live video accusing a Brunswick County Sheriff's Office deputy of racism after she was ordered to sign a summons asking her to appear in court or prepay a traffic ticket.

"I have had a traumatic experience, and I want the people who are not African-American who know me to really get where we are coming from," Hilton-Williams says. "When I saw the police pull up behind me, the state trooper, I was immediately afraid. ...

"This is the area," she says, moving the camera to show the rural road. "In the middle of this kind of stuff. This is where I am, so it's not like I'm not afraid, because this is where we got lynched. ... Do any of my white friends ... feel like that when they get pulled over?" Hilton-Williams says the "bully" cop "threatened" to "pull her out" of the car for refusing to sign the ticket and was "degrading" her "as an African-American." Her Facebook footage—taken right after she was stopped—was widely shared.

But the body cam video tells a different story. The officer, addressing her as "Ma'am," explains he clocked her going 70 mph on a rural highway that has a 55 mph limit. Asked to sign the summons for speeding, she repeatedly refuses. The officer explains: "What you are signing here is a promise to come to court or a promise to prepay. It's not an admission of guilt. ... If you refuse to sign the summons, at this point, I'm going to have to get you outside of this car, I'm going to place you under arrest and take you in front of a magistrate. I will get your vehicle towed. ... You do not have a choice but to sign this summons. So once again, you're signing right there. So thank you. I knew you were going to sign it. Thank you very much. ... Have a very safe day."

Third, a viral post last week by civil rights "activist" Shaun King claimed that in Ellis County, Texas, a Texas Department of Public Safety trooper sexually assaulted a black woman, Sherita Dixon-Cole, following a traffic stop, then arrested her for driving while intoxicated. King wrote: "The officer first communicated to Sherita that he would be willing to let her go if she performed sexual favors for him, then proceeded to sexually assault her, touching her under her skirt," King said in an interview. But two days later, the TDPS released a nearly two-hour body cam video and issued the following statement: "The video shows absolutely no evidence to support the egregious and unsubstantiated accusations against the Trooper during the DWI arrest of the suspect. The Department is appalled that anyone would make such a despicable, slanderous and false accusation."

When a cop is caught on tape mistreating a suspect, many say, "Imagine what would've happened had this not been filmed by a civilian with a smartphone." But this cuts both ways. How often do civilians falsely accuse police officers of misconduct?

If Tough Anti-Drug Laws Are 'Racist,' Blame Black Leaders

June 14, 2018

Why did Alice Marie Johnson, a first-time nonviolent drug offender, get a life sentence? She and her husband divorced in 1989. The next year, she lost her job as a FedEx manager, followed by bankruptcy and home foreclosure in 1991. The following year, the mother of five lost her youngest child in a tragic motorcycle accident. She says the emotional and financial pressure caused her to make the "biggest mistake of (her) life." By her own admission, she "became what is called a telephone mule ... passing messages between the distributors and sellers ... in a drug conspiracy." She and 15 others were arrested in 1993 for drug trafficking and money laundering.

While many of her co-defendants were given reduced or dropped charges for cooperating with prosecutors, Johnson was convicted for cocaine conspiracy and money laundering in 1996, and sentenced to mandatory life in prison without parole, plus an additional 25 years.

In the '80s and '90s, many black leaders supported tough anti-drug laws. Facing an inner-city explosion of gang activity, violent crime and a crack epidemic, black politicians pressured Congress to pass these laws. The Rev. George McMurray was pastor of Harlem's Mother A.M.E. Zion Church in the '70s, a time when New York City faced a major heroin epidemic. He favored life sentences for convicted drug dealers. "When you send a few men to prison for life, someone's going to pass the word down, 'It's not too good over here,'" McMurray said. "So instead of robbery and selling dope, (they'll think) 'I want to go to school and live a good life.'"

When President Ronald Reagan signed the Anti-Drug Abuse Act of 1986 into law—the law that punished crack cocaine dealers far more harshly than powder cocaine dealers—Harlem's Rep. Charlie Rangel stood right behind Reagan. Crack dealers, many of whom were black, got harsher sentences than those who dealt powder cocaine, many of whom were white. And Congressional Black Caucus members pushed Reagan to create the Office of National Drug Control Policy.

Then came the massive 1994 Violent Crime Control and Law Enforcement Act, which included longer sentences for first-time offenders. An influential group of black pastors wrote to the Congressional Black Caucus, "While we do not agree with every provision in the crime bill, we do believe and emphatically support the bill's goal to save our communities, and most importantly, our children."

The black mayor of Baltimore, Kurt Schmoke, said: "I believe the crime bill ... is part of the answer, and the crime bill should be supported by us. We do need to send a signal throughout our communities that certain types of activities will not be tolerated, that people will be held accountable and that if there is evil manifested by actions taken by individuals who choose to prey upon our residents that that evil will be responded to quickly and correctly." The majority of the Congressional Black Caucus supported Congress' final bill. President Bill Clinton signed it. Hillary Clinton defended the crime bill a couple years later, saying that these laws were necessary to combat "superpredators"—a comment that came back to haunt her during the 2016 presidential campaign.

But after black crack dealers received longer sentences than whites who dealt powder, the 1986 law became "racist." The CBC later asked President Bill Clinton to fix the disparity. His sentencing commission also advised him to narrow the disparity. Clinton, who wanted to appear "tough on drugs," refused. So when Clinton signed his own tough anti-drug law in 1995, it preserved the crack-powder disparity. The Los Angeles Times wrote: "One week after President Clinton decried the 'disproportionate percentage' of young black men going to prison, he has decided to sign into law a bill that would maintain stiff prison sentences for those caught with small amounts of crack cocaine."

President Donald Trump challenged the kneeling NFL players to give him names of those who have been "unfairly treated" by our criminal justice system. He promised to set up a process to review their cases and either pardon them or commute their sentences. It's a heck of an offer and should be a no-brainer. Given Colin Kaepernick and other NFL players' assertions of institutional/systemic/structural racism, Trump should soon be deluged with names of worthy candidates. If, as alleged, cops bust blacks for reasons of "racial profiling" and if, as alleged, blacks are wrongfully convicted and sentenced, how can the NFL players turn down Trump's offer?

But to assert that black convicts like Alice Johnson are victims of a "racist" criminal justice system ignores the role played by black members of Congress to pass the very laws later denounced as racist.

IG Report—Imagine This Level of Bias During the O.J. Simpson Case

June 21, 2018

Imagine what defense attorney Johnnie Cochran, during the O.J. Simpson murder trial, would have done with notes to and from LAPD lead detectives Tom Lange and Philip Vannatter in which they demeaned Simpson's fans. Imagine a written exchange in which one detective said, "We'll stop him!" Imagine Cochran's opening and closing arguments, to say nothing of his cross-examination, if he'd had evidence similar to the kind of bias found in the Department of Justice inspector general's report on the FBI's handling of the Hillary Clinton email investigation.

The DOJ IG report included several messages between FBI attorneys and employees who worked on the email investigation. Here is one from an unidentified FBI employee (who didn't work on the email investigation) to FBI attorneys, the day after Trump's election: "I can't stop crying. ... You promised me this wouldn't happen. YOU PROMISED. ... Trump's supporters are all poor to middle class, uneducated, lazy POS that think he will magically grant them jobs for doing nothing. They probably didn't watch the debates, aren't fully educated on his policies, and are stupidly wrapped up in his unmerited enthusiasm."

This is an Aug. 8, 2016, text message exchange between an FBI investigator—who was helping lead the investigation into Russia's interference in the election at the time—and an FBI senior attorney, who were both married to other people and having an affair with each other. In the message, released to the public for the first time, FBI attorney Lisa Page wrote: "(Trump's) not ever going to become president, right? Right?!" "No. No he won't. We'll stop it," said lead agent Peter Strzok.

Yet, incredibly, the IG concluded that political bias did not influence the outcome of the investigation. The report said: "We did not find documentary or testimonial evidence that improper considerations, including political bias, directly affected the specific investigative actions we reviewed."

Still, when IG Michael Horowitz testified about his report, as ex-CBS News reporter Sharyl Attkisson notes, Horowitz used many double negatives: "What we say here is not ... that there was no bias." As to FBI lead investigator Peter Strzok's prioritizing the Trump/Russia collusion investigation over the Clinton email probe, Horowitz said, "We were not convinced that that was not a biased decision."

Horowitz also said this about Strzok's bias: "The one area where we were concerned about bias was in the October time period, and the ... weighing of Agent Strzok between focusing on the Russia investigation versus the Weiner laptop (Clinton emails), and our concern about his decision given the text messages."

Consider this exchange between Sen. Mike Crapo, R-Idaho, and Horowitz:

Crapo: "What you're telling us is you found bias; those who you found the bias among said, 'Well, we didn't let it bleed into our work performance,' and you don't have evidence to disprove that."

Horowitz: "Correct."

The IG report said: "When one senior FBI official, Strzok, who was helping to lead the Russia investigation at the time, conveys in a text message to another senior FBI official, Page, that 'we'll stop' candidate Trump from being elected—after other extensive text messages between the two disparaging candidate Trump—it is not only indicative of a biased state of mind but, even more seriously, implies a willingness to take official action to impact the presidential candidate's electoral prospects. This is antithetical to the core values of the FBI and the Department of Justice."

Simpson defense attorney Cochran vilified white cop Mark Fuhrman as a "genocidal racist." What made Fuhrman a "genocidal racist"? Fuhrman, the "dream team" learned, used the N-word a number of times while discussing his police work in a taped conversation with a screenwriter *seven years earlier*. And three witnesses testified that Fuhrman used the N-word in conversations with them in the mid-1980s.

Imagine if witnesses had credibly testified that, during the investigation, they heard Fuhrman calling Simpson and/or his fans "deplorables" or "uneducated, lazy POS."

In fact, during the O.J. Simpson case, then-LAPD Chief Willie Williams, who happened to be black, ordered a report to determine whether any bias or misconduct affected the integrity of their investigation. Some investigators, the report found, made minor procedural errors. But the report found neither evidence of bias against Simpson nor evidence of misconduct by any of the investigators, let alone any bias or misconduct that affected the judgment of the investigators.

Now suppose the LAPD report had noted numerous instances of bias and demeaning remarks by several investigators toward Simpson, yet the report nevertheless concluded, "We did not find documentary or testimonial evidence that improper considerations, including political bias, directly affected the specific investigative actions we reviewed."

Seriously?

Criminal Behavior, Not Racism, Explains 'Racial Disparities' in Crime Stats

June 28, 2018

A new study on racial disparities in police conduct found that differences in offending by suspects, not racism, explains officers' responses.

In the study "Is There Evidence of Racial Disparity in Police Use of Deadly Force?" professors from Michigan State and Arizona State universities analyzed officer-involved fatal shootings in 2015 and 2016. The report's abstract says: "We benchmark two years of fatal shooting data on 16 crime rate estimates. When adjusting for crime, we find no systematic evidence of anti-black disparities in fatal shootings, fatal shootings of unarmed citizens, or fatal shootings involving misidentification of harmless objects. ... Exposure to police given crime rate differences likely accounts for the higher per capita rate of fatal police shootings for blacks, at least when analyzing all shootings. For unarmed shootings or misidentification shootings, data are too uncertain to be conclusive."

Two recent studies found cops *more reluctant* to use deadly force against blacks, including one by a black Harvard economist. Professor Roland G. Fryer Jr. concluded: "On the most extreme use of force—officer-involved shootings—we find no racial differences in either the raw data or when contextual factors are taken into account."

But aren't blacks routinely "racially profiled" by cops? Not according to the Police-Public Contact Survey. Produced every three years by the Department of Justice's Bureau of Justice Statistics, the survey asks more than 60,000 people about their interactions with the police. It asks respondents' to provide age, race and gender. It asks them whether they had any contact with the police in the last year; what was the experience like; how were your treated; was there a use of force and so on. Turns out, according to a September 2017 National Review article, black men and white men are about equally likely to have a contact with a cop in a given year. As to multiple contacts, defined as three or more with the police in a given year, 1.5 percent of blacks vs. 1.2 percent of whites fall in that category. Not much difference.

There's also the National Crime Victimization Survey, which questions victims of crimes, whether or not the criminal was captured, as to the race and ethnicity of the suspect. It turns out that the race of the arrested matches the percentage given by victims. So unless victims are lying about the race of their assailant, unconcerned about whether he gets caught, blacks are not being "overarrested."

A reasonable discussion about blacks and police practices cannot take place without acknowledging the disproportion amount of crime committed by blacks. According to the Department of Justice's "Felony Defendants in Large Urban Counties, 2009," in the country's 75 largest counties, blacks committed 62 percent of robberies, 45 percent of assaults and accounted for 57 percent of murder defendants.

The No. 1 cause of preventable death for young white men is accidents, such as car accidents. The No. 1 cause of preventable death for young black men is homicide, usually committed by another young black man, not a cop. In 2016, according to the latest data from the FBI's Uniform Crime Report, 7,881 blacks were killed.

The courageous Manhattan Institute's Heather Mac Donald, who writes extensively about police practice, asked: "Who is killing these black victims? Not whites, and not the police, but other blacks. In 2016, the police fatally shot 233 blacks, the vast majority armed and dangerous. ... Contrary to the Black Lives Matter narrative, the police have much more to fear from black males than black males have to fear from the police. In 2015, a police officer was 18.5 times more likely to be killed by a black male than an unarmed black male was to be killed by a police officer."

In 2012 in the city of Rialto, California, population approximately 100,000, cops were randomly assigned body cameras based on their shifts. Over the next year, use-of-force incidents on the shifts that had cameras were half the rate of those without cameras. But something rather extraordinary also happened. Complaints against all Rialto police officers with were down almost 90 percent from the prior year.

It turns out when civilians knew they were being recorded, they—not the cops—behaved better and stop making false accusations. The use of force by cops also declined, but, again, not because the police changed their conduct. No, the cops continued performing as they'd been trained. Civilians, aware that they were being taped, were less confrontational and were more likely to cooperate and follow instructions. As a result, cops needed to use force less frequently.

Still, when actor Jesse Williams gave a four-minute rant at the 2016 BET Awards about what he considered racist police practices, he claimed, "What we've been doing is looking at the data, and we know that police somehow manage to de-escalate, disarm and not kill white people every day."

Trump Blamed for Death of Reporters: Did Media Blame Obama for Cop Killers?

July 5, 2018

A man with a long-standing beef against the Annapolis, Maryland, newspaper Capital Gazette entered the paper's headquarters with a shotgun and murdered five staffers. It represents the deadliest attack on U.S. reporters in modern history.

Before learning about the suspect's mental issues and his long-standing feud with the newspaper, some in the media blamed President Donald Trump. After all, critics said, Trump routinely denounces "fake news" as an existential threat to our republic. Connect the dots, they said. Blame Trump! CNN aired a montage of Trump's attacks on the media. Rob Cox, a Reuters editor, tweeted: "This is what happens when @RealDonaldTrump calls journalists the enemy of the people. Blood is on your hands, Mr. President." Another reporter, who later resigned, even falsely tweeted that the shooter was wearing a MAGA cap. How do you get *that* wrong?

How dare the President call out the anti-Republican media for its decades of biased reporting? Pew Research, in 2013, found that only 7 percent of reporters called themselves Republican. How dare Trump attack The New York Times, which has not endorsed a Republican presidential candidate since 1956? How dare Trump go after The Washington Post, which has *never* endorsed a Republican presidential candidate. And how dare Trump refer to CNN—one of whose "news" anchors, Don Lemon, has called Trump "a racist"—as fake news.

Did the media hold President Barack Obama responsible for the murders of 10 cops in Dallas, Baton Rouge and New York City, all at the hands of black men apparently incited by their belief that cops murder blacks without consequence? After all, Obama frequently criticized the police and bemoaned America's racism as "part of our DNA."

President Obama's anti-cop rhetoric started right after he took office. Obama's friend, a black Harvard professor, was arrested in his home. Professor Henry Louis Gates, back from a trip, couldn't open his front door and reportedly asked his driver to help. A neighbor, observing two people trying to force open the front door of Gates' home, called 911. But when the cops arrived and asked Gates to exit the home so he could determine its ownership, Gates mouthed off and was briefly arrested. Obama said, "The Cambridge police acted stupidly." The Cambridge Police Superior Officers Association and the Cambridge Police commissioner insisted the officer followed protocol. Obama's statement infuriated officers all across the country and set up a template for the Obama administration: Cops engage in unlawful anti-black racial profiling.

Obama and his attorney general also offered verbal support to the so-called Black Lives Matter movement that argues, without facts, that blacks are regularly and illegally profiled by an institutionally, systemically and structurally "racist" criminal justice system. It did not help that during the first six years of the Obama administration, the anti-police incendiary Rev. Al Sharpton, according to The Washington Post, visited the White House 72 times. What kind of message did *that* send to the police?

When a Sanford, Florida, neighborhood watch captain, George Zimmerman, shot and killed a black 17-year-old named Trayvon Martin, President Obama promptly sided with the deceased teen, saying, "If I had a son, he'd look like Trayvon." A jury found Zimmerman not guilty, and one juror later said that during the deliberations, race never came up.

Then there's Ferguson. A grim President Obama, at an address before the United Nations, said: "In a summer marked by instability in the Middle East and Eastern Europe, I know the world also took notice of the small American city of Ferguson, Missouri—where a young man was killed, and a community was divided. So yes, we have our own racial and ethnic tensions."

But the Ferguson grand jury did not indict the officer who shot and killed Michael Brown, and a Department of Justice report exonerated the cop. Contrary to the lies told by his friend who witnessed the shooting,

Michael Brown did *not* have his hands up when the officer shot and killed him. Brown, did not say, "Hands up. Don't shoot." Yet before the investigation even began, Obama's BFF, Sharpton, took to the streets of Ferguson yelling, "No justice, no peace."

The DOJ's investigation of Ferguson's nearly all-white police department criticized its alleged "institutional racism." But its actual findings do not support that conclusion. Ferguson, the investigation noted, is 67 percent black, but 85 percent of its traffic stops involve black drivers. To the DOJ, this 18-point statistical imbalance equals systemic racism. But in New York City, where the department consists mostly officers of color, 55 percent of traffic stops involve a black driver in a city with a 25 percent black population. This is a 30-point statistical imbalance. Wouldn't this make the NYPD even more "institutionally racist" than the Ferguson PD?

Trump, say the media, has created an atmosphere that puts reporters in danger. Obama often unfairly criticized the police. But the media did not blame Obama for the murder of officers by angry black men consumed with the wrongheaded belief that blacks are victimized by the "institutional racism" of the criminal justice system.

Slavery: What They Didn't Teach in My High School

July 12, 2018

A man I have known since grade school changed his name, years ago, to an Arabic one. He told me he rejected Christianity as "the white man's religion that justified slavery." He argued Africans taken out of that continent were owed reparations. "From whom?" I asked.

Arab slavers took more Africans out of Africa and transported them to the Middle East and to South America than European slavers took out of Africa and brought to North America. Arab slavers began taking slaves out of Africa beginning in the ninth century—centuries before the European slave trade—and continued well after.

In "Prisons & Slavery," John Dewar Gleissner writes: "The Arabs' treatment of black Africans can aptly be termed an African Holocaust. Arabs killed more Africans in transit, especially when crossing the Sahara Desert, than Europeans and Americans, and over more centuries, both before and after the years of the Atlantic slave trade. Arab Muslims began extracting millions of black African slaves centuries before Christian nations did. Arab slave traders removed slaves from Africa for about 13 centuries, compared to three centuries of the Atlantic slave trade. African slaves transported by Arabs across the Sahara Desert died more often than slaves making the Middle Passage to the New World by ship. Slaves invariably died within five years if they worked in the Ottoman Empire's Sahara salt mines."

My name-changing friend did not know that slavery occurred on every continent except Antarctica. Europeans enslaved other Europeans. Asians enslaved Asians. Africans enslaved other Africans. Arabs enslaved other Arabs. Native Americans even enslaved other Native Americans.

He accused me of "relying on white historians" who, he insisted, had a "vested interest to lie."

What about Thomas Sowell, the brilliant/economist/historian/philosopher, who happens to be black? Sowell writes: "Of all the tragic facts about the history of slavery, the most astonishing to an American today is that, although slavery was a worldwide institution for thousands of years, nowhere in the world was slavery a controversial issue prior to the 18th century.

"People of every race and color were enslaved—and enslaved others. White people were still being bought and sold as slaves in the Ottoman Empire, decades after American blacks were freed."

Sowell also wrote: "The region of West Africa ... was one of the great slave-trading regions of the continent—before, during, and after the white man arrived. It was the Africans who enslaved their fellow Africans, selling some of these slaves to Europeans or to Arabs and keeping others for themselves. Even at the peak of the Atlantic slave trade, Africans retained more slaves for themselves than they sent to the Western Hemisphere. ... Arabs were the leading slave raiders in East Africa, ranging over an area larger than all of Europe."

I asked my friend if his anger over slavery extended to countries like Brazil. "Brazil?" he said.

Harvard's Department of African and African American Studies professor Henry Louis Gates Jr.—who also happens to be black—wrote: "Between 1525 and 1866, in the entire history of the slave trade to the New World, according to the Trans-Atlantic Slave Trade Database, 12.5 *million* Africans were shipped to the New World. 10.7 million survived the dreaded Middle Passage, disembarking in North America, the Caribbean and South America. And how many of these 10.7 million Africans were shipped directly to North America? *Only about 388,000.* That's right: a tiny percentage. In fact, the overwhelming percentage of the African slaves were shipped directly to the Caribbean and South America; Brazil received *4.86 million Africans alone!*"

African tribes who captured other tribes *sold* them into slavery. For this reason, in 2006, Ghana offered an official apology. Emmanuel Hagan, director of research and statistics at Ghana's Ministry of Tourism and Diaspora Relations, explains: "The reason why we wanted to do some formal thing is that we want—even if it's just for the surface of it, for the cosmetic of it—to be seen to be saying 'sorry' to those who feel very strongly and who we believe have distorted history, because they get the impression that it was people here who just took them and sold them. It's something we have to look straight in the face and try to address, because it exists. So we will want to say something went wrong. People made mistakes, but we are sorry for whatever happened."

Over 600,000 Americans, in a country with less than 10 percent of today's population, died in the Civil War that ended slavery. "While slavery was common to all civilizations," writes Sowell, "...only one civilization developed a moral revulsion against it, very late in its history—Western civilization. ... Not even the leading moralists in other civilizations rejected slavery at all."

And, no, after all this, my friend did not reconsider his name change.

Russian Bots vs. Media/Academia/Hollywood—Which Had a Bigger Impact on the Election?

July 19, 2018

The indictment of a dozen Russian spies explained, in great detail, the extent of their interference in the 2016 election. Americans learned about the depth and extent of the Russian operation to interfere.

That the Russian activity altered the outcome of the election to "make Trump win" has become an article of faith for many who still cannot fathom how Donald Trump beat Hillary Clinton. This will persist as a subject of speculation in book after book, for a long time. What will be of less concern to the same researchers and writers is the *far* greater impact of the anti-Trump trio of media, academia and Hollywood.

Professor Tim Groseclose, author of "Left Turn: How Liberal Media Bias Distorts the American Mind," makes the case that were the media truly fair and balanced, the average state would vote the same way Texas votes, in favor of Republicans. But media bias gives Democrats a bump of about 8 to 10 points. Of 20 major sources of news, Groseclose found about 15 years ago, 90 percent lean to the left.

The late Barbara Bush said she was surprised when her son won the presidency in 2000: "I just thought it's too difficult. And you're not going to like this, but my gut feeling is that all the media is against George, Republicans, any Republican." That Democrats and liberals in the media outnumber Republicans and conservatives is a fact. Years ago, the Pew Research Center conducted a survey of over 500 national reporters, editors and media executives and found that only 7 percent self-identified as "conservative." Most of the major newspapers endorsed Clinton over Trump. The New York Times hasn't endorsed a Republican for president since 1956. The Washington Post, which has only been endorsing presidents for 42 years, has *never* endorsed a Republican.

NBC's "Meet the Press" host Chuck Todd worked on the 1992 presidential campaign of left-left Democrat Sen. Tom Harkin. CNN's Jake Tapper used to work for a U.S. House Democrat. ABC News "chief anchor" George Stephanopoulos worked as a top campaign strategist for the election of Bill Clinton, and after Clinton's election worked as his communications director.

Critics at CNN hyperventilate over the relationship between President Trump and Sean Hannity. CNN's Brian Stelter called this relationship between the star of a television news network and the president "weird," saying, "No TV host has ever had this kind of relationship with a U.S. president before." Really? Hannity is not a news "journalist," and the relationship is not a secret. Contrast this with the close relationship President John Kennedy enjoyed with Ben Bradlee, the editor of the highly influential Washington Post, the paper that helped topple President Richard Nixon. That the two were close is no secret. What the public did not know is that Bradlee was such an advocate for JFK that, during the primary presidential campaign, Bradlee gave Kennedy private tips on how to beat rival Lyndon Johnson.

The Huffington Post, for months after Trump's formal entry into the race, refused to cover the campaign in its political section. Publisher Arianna Huffington called Trump's candidacy, in effect, a circus that did not deserve serious coverage.

Academia, on the humanities side, overwhelmingly leans left. What effect does this have on the voting habits of students? Since Trump's election, we've seen a video of a university teacher likening Trump voters to "terrorists." We hear of professors denouncing Trump as "racist" and predicting a dystopian future. No doubt during the election many professors let their opinions and preferences be known to their students. Years ago, an American Enterprise magazine study confirmed what we already know, that our college and university faculty, whether big or small, north or south, east or west, private or public, are mostly left-wing. What effect does our left-wing academia have on the electorate?

Hollywood hates Trump. From first dismissing candidate Trump as a clown and a buffoon to, post-election, when actor Robert De Niro said,

"F--- Trump," Hollywood dislikes Trump perhaps even more than it did President George W. Bush over the Iraq War and Hurricane Katrina.

Ann Coulter was ridiculed by "Real Time" host Bill Maher, her co-panelists and the studio audience when she told Bill Maher that she thought Trump could win the Republican nomination. President Barack Obama, echoing a common line throughout the election from the late-night comics, insisted Trump would never be president.

There is no doubt that Russia attempted to interfere in our 2016 presidential election. Why didn't Obama do more to stop it? Two likely reasons. First, Obama correctly assumed that the American people could not be manipulated into voting for someone they otherwise didn't want to because Russian bots reprogrammed their minds through Facebook. Second, Obama, like most pundits, assumed that Hillary Clinton, whom he called the "most qualified" candidate ever to run, was unbeatable.

Whatever influence Russia may have had on the elections is dwarfed by the "collusion" of the largely anti-GOP media, academia and Hollywood. If the right dominated these fields, congressional Democrats would demand hearings.

Trump Skeptical About 'Official Government Findings'? Who Isn't?

July 26, 2018

President Donald Trump, in Helsinki, expressed skepticism about the intelligence community's finding that Russia interfered with the 2016 presidential election. Within 24 hours, the President walked back his skepticism and said he trusts the intel community and believes their finding that Russia interfered with the 2016 election.

But the Helsinki hysteria continued.

Some Trump cable critics pronounced him "treasonous." How dare the President waffle on the intelligence community's definitive conclusion that Russia meddled? It's "treasonous" to be guarded about official government conclusions? We're going to need more prisons to house all the offenders.

After all, this is the same crowd that believed President George W. Bush "lied us into the Iraq war," despite Bush's reliance on the unanimous opinion of our intelligence agencies. A recent Huffington Post/YouGov survey found that 56 percent of Democrats still believe "Bush did ... lie about weapons of mass destruction in order to get the U.S. into the Iraq War." To believe this, Democrats must therefore reject the conclusion of the bipartisan Robb-Silberman commission report, which uncovered deeply flawed intelligence but no intention to deceive.

About Helsinki, CNN's Anderson Cooper called Trump's remarks "one of the most disgraceful moments by an American President on the world stage." Really? And where does Cooper rank the performance of President Barack Obama, who invoked the lie of Ferguson while addressing the United Nations? Before the investigation was concluded, Obama said: "I know the world also took notice of the small American city of Ferguson, Missouri—where a young man was killed. ... So yes, we have our own racial and ethnic tensions." The investigation ultimately concluded that the officer used justifiable force and the suspect did not have his hands up and did not say, "Don't shoot."

Some cable news hosts wondered why Trump's Cabinet members failed to resign in protest over Trump's alleged lack of respect for the intelligence community. Do they mean the way President Bill Clinton's Cabinet reacted after he called them into the Oval Office, told them he did not have an affair with Monica Lewinsky and sent cabinet members like Secretary of State Madeleine Albright out to assert, "We believe the allegations against the President are untrue"? Yet, when the semen-stained blue dress later proved that Clinton lied to and used them, *no one resigned!*

As for Trump's skepticism about government findings, a 2013 Washington Post/ABC News poll found that most Americans reject the lone-gunman conclusion of the Warren Commission, which investigated the assassination of President John F. Kennedy. Even Robert Kennedy reportedly told friends that he doubted the commission's conclusion.

What about racial conspiracy theories believed by otherwise intelligent people?

Missouri's Claire McCaskill, while running for the U.S. Senate, said, "(President) George (W.) Bush let people die on rooftops in New Orleans because they were poor and because they were black." Nation of Islam Minister Louis Farrakhan publicly accused President Bush of intentionally blowing up levees in New Orleans. Filmmaker Spike Lee also helped to peddle that ridiculous narrative. The Washington Post's columnist Eugene Robinson said there were "reasonable, sober people who really believe that (levees were intentionally blown up)."

The so-called "Black Lives Matter" movement is based upon the lie that the police routinely engage in racial profiling against blacks, despite numerous government studies disproving the "racial profiling" narrative vigorously promoted by social justice activists, left-wing cable channels and politicians who want blacks angry so that they vote Democrat.

Despite a House Select Committee's persuasive finding that a lone gunman, James Earl Ray, assassinated Martin Luther King Jr., some King family members disagreed. King's youngest son, Dexter, accepted Ray's claim of innocence, visited him in prison and even shook his hand! Dexter King said to Ray: "Well, as awkward as this may seem, I want you to know that I believe you and my family believes you, and we are going to do everything in our power to try and make sure that justice will prevail. And while it's at the 11th hour, I've always been a spiritual person and I believe in Providence."

As to rejecting the conclusions of government reports, during the O.J. Simpson double homicide case, the LAPD was led by Willie Williams, the department's first black police chief. Because of the constant and serious allegations of evidence planting, Chief Williams ordered an investigation. The probe found no evidence of any evidence planting or other intentional acts by cops, criminalists or investigators to compromise the case. Nevertheless, the polls continued to show that most blacks, at the time, believed O.J. Simpson was "innocent." The "free O.J. crowd" could not have cared less about Williams' report.

So add Trump to the list of Americans who are skeptical about some government findings, less so about others. But as for people who *still* claim "Bush lied, people died" and who *still* consider O.J. Simpson an innocent man "framed by the racist LAPD"—pray for them, and keep them away from sharp objects.

Anne Hathaway Is Making 'Race Relations' Worse

August 2, 2018

Dear Ms. Anne Hathaway,

Two black sisters at an Oakland, California, subway station were attacked by a knife-wielding white man. He killed one sister, Nia Wilson, and injured the other. The Bay Area Rapid Transit police arrested him. His family reportedly told authorities that he suffered from mental problems. The authorities say that, for now, no evidence suggests that the suspect was motivated by race.

But you did not need to wait for evidence of a hate crime, something you insist blacks worry about from sunup to sunset. You wrote: "(Wilson's murder) is unspeakable and MUST NOT BE MET with silence. ... She was a black woman and she was murdered in cold blood by a white man. White people—including me, including you—must take into the marrow of our privileged bones the truth that ALL black people fear for their lives DAILY in America and have done so for GENERATIONS. ... We must ask our (white)selves—how 'decent' are we really? Not in our intent, but in our actions? In our lack of action?"

Ms. Hathaway, you are no doubt well-intentioned, but you're not helping.

True, an NBC News/Survey Monkey poll in May found that most Americans think race relations are getting worse. But 47 percent say they "rarely" or "never" discuss race relations with friends and family. Americans agree that race relations are bad, yet they don't discuss it with friends and family? Perhaps it's because the perception that race relations are bad is stronger than the reality.

After Dylann Roof murdered several black churchgoers in Charleston, South Carolina, then-Democratic presidential candidate Martin O'Malley said the mass murder shows the additional work America must undertake to improve race relations. But when asked specifically what should be done, O'Malley, the former mayor of Baltimore and governor of Maryland, stammered before finally admitting, "I don't know exactly how we, how we, how we address this."

In fact, hate crimes represent a tiny fraction of 1 percent of all crimes committed. As for offenders in hate crimes where the offenders' race is known, blacks are overrepresented. In 2016, the latest year for which statistics are available, blacks, at 13 percent of the population, committed 26.1 percent of hate crimes. Whites, at over 75 percent of the population, committed 46.3 percent of hate crimes. This figure of hate crimes committed by whites is likely overstated because these percentages include white Hispanics.

You imply that blacks are disproportionately hurt by white-on-black violent crime. In 2015, Ann Coulter wrote: "In 2008, the most recent year for which such data seems to have been collected, FBI surveys show that, out of 520,161 interracial violent crimes, blacks committed 429,444 of them against whites, while whites committed 90,717 of them against blacks. In other words, blacks commit more than 80 percent of all interracial violent crime." Economist John Lott wrote in 2014, "Black male teenagers were nine times more likely to commit murders than similarly aged white males." And almost always the murderer of a young black male is another young black male.

How bad is it for blacks in America?

A 1997 Time/CNN poll shows more black teens than white believe that "failure to take advantage of available opportunities" was a bigger problem than racism. And 89 percent of black teens said that racism was a small problem or no problem in their own daily lives.

A 1995 Washington Post poll found that middle-income blacks believed Hispanics and Asians were plagued by more anti-Hispanic and anti-Asian discrimination than did Hispanics and Asians.

A 2013 Rasmussen poll of blacks, whites and Hispanics asked which of these three groups is the most racist. Whites said blacks. Hispanics said blacks. Blacks said blacks. Twenty years ago, a poll commissioned by the Anti-Defamation League found that 34 percent of blacks were anti-Semitic, nearly four times higher than the percentage of whites considered anti-Semitic.

The NFL's Colin Kaepernick and other players refused to stand for the national anthem over the alleged systemic mistreatment of blacks by the criminal justice system. President Donald Trump said: "I'm going to ask all of those people to recommend to me—because that's what they're protesting—people that they think were unfairly treated by the justice system ... if ... they've been unfairly treated then we'll pardon them. Or at least let them out." That was nearly two months ago. *Where's the list of names?*

Ms. Hathaway, if you really want to improve black-white "race relations," here's some advice you might dispense: Comply with cops to avoid getting killed; work hard; advocate for school choice; "kids, do your homework"; at least finish high school; get married before having a child; and save and invest.

At the very least, please understand that by telling black people they "fear for their lives daily" due to murderous whites, you're not helping. Racism has long diminished as a major problem in America. The institutional/systemic/structural racism narrative is driven by the mainstream racism-obsessed media, Democrats seeking black votes, "activists" and the well-intentioned but misinformed—but not by the facts on the ground.

The New York Times Hires Left-Wing Bigot for Its Editorial Board

August 9, 2018

The New York Times, for its editorial board, hired a 30-year-old tech writer named Sarah Jeong, an American immigrant from South Korea. But Jeong, only a few years ago, posted a series of offensive, anti-white tweets.

Her anti-white tweets included the following:

"Dumbass f-ing white people marking up the internet with their opinions like dogs pissing on fire hydrants."

"Oh man it's kind of sick how much joy I get out of being cruel to old white men."

"I dare you to get on Wikipedia and play 'Things white people can definitely take credit for, it's really hard."

"Are white people genetically predisposed to burn faster in the sun, thus logically being only fit to live underground like groveling goblins(?)"

The New York Times stands by its decision. You see, said The New York Times in a statement, Jeong was merely being sarcastic. She was actually mocking the racism of her twitter detractors. She was, in effect, trolling the trolls. The Times said: "Her journalism and the fact that she is a young Asian woman have made her a subject of frequent online harassment. For a period of time she responded to that harassment by imitating the rhetoric of her harassers. She sees now that this approach only served to feed the vitriol that we too often see on social media. She regrets it, and The Times does not condone it."

As defenses go, The New York Times' defense of its new editorial board hire is creative. But what about Jeong's anti-cop and anti-male tweets? Here's a sample:

"Cops are assholes."

"Let me know when a cop gets killed by a rock or molotov cocktail or a stray shard of glass from a precious precious window."

"If we're talking big sweeping bans on s--- that kills people, why don't we ever ever ever ever talk about banning the police?"

"I SURE WOULD FIGHT THE COPS WITH MY GUNS, I WONDER WHY BLACK PEOPLE HAVEN'T THOUGHT OF THAT."

"My point is that we should kill all the men *prior* to removing the state from marriage as an institution."

Was Jeong still being satirical when she attacked cops, too?

In an earnings call last November, John Schnatter, the founder of Papa John's, gave the following analysis of why his company's third-quarter earnings were disappointing. Schnatter said: "The NFL has hurt us. ... We are disappointed the NFL and its leadership did not resolve this." He was referring to the NFL national anthem player protests, which he insisted should have been "nipped in the bud" the previous year. Schnatter said, "Leadership starts at the top, and this is an example of poor leadership."

Critics called his comments "racist" because most of the players in the NFL are black, as are most of the protestors. Therefore, Schnatter was being racist by objecting to the mostly black kneelers. Schnatter apologized, but Papa John's stock tumbled after Schnatter's NFL comment, and in January, Schnatter stepped down as CEO.

Schnatter eventually resigned as chairman of the board for something he said months later. In a May telephone conference call about how his company can be more racially tolerant and sensitive, Schnatter reportedly defended his November NFL comments by stating, "Colonel Sanders called blacks n-----s," yet, claimed Schnatter, never faced public backlash. Schnatter was out. Never mind his claim that he was quoting someone else during a role-playing exercise.

Roseanne Barr, a few months ago, lost her show because of a "racist" tweet about former Obama White House aide and consultant, Valerie Jarrett. Barr tweeted: "muslim brotherhood & planet of the apes had a baby=vj." Barr claimed she did not know Jarrett was black, making her tweet offensive, argued Barr, but not racist.

As for Jeong, a CNN political commentator claimed that it is impossible for Jeong to be racist. Symone Sanders says racism requires power. Sanders apparently believes that only white men possess power and therefore a woman of Korean heritage is incapable of racism. Sanders said, "Being racist is not just prejudice, it's prejudice plus power. So one could argue that some of her tweets, even within context, note that she has a prejudice, perhaps, against white men, but that, in fact, does not make her racist. I don't think she is a racist. ... Could she have some not just implicit, but, you know, negative bias toward white men in America due to perhaps what she is experienced throughout her life?"

Contrast Sanders' definition of racism with that of The New York Times' columnist Charles Blow. In an article about President Donald Trump's alleged racism, Blow said: "Racism is simply the belief that race is an inherent and determining factor in a person's or a people's character and capabilities, rendering some inferior and others superior."

Trump's Hollywood Star Must Go—But They Get a Pass?

August 16, 2018

During the 2016 presidential campaign, a man dressed like a construction worker, carrying a pickax, destroyed Donald Trump's sidewalk star on the Hollywood Walk of Fame. The Hollywood Chamber of Commerce promptly replaced it. Just three weeks ago, a different man, presumably with a different pickax, also destroyed Trump's star.

Meanwhile, the neighboring West Hollywood City Council (an independent city) passed a unanimous resolution urging the Hollywood Chamber of Commerce (which selects who receives a star) and the City of Los Angeles (where the public sidewalk tourist attraction resides) to remove the star.

The resolution read: "Starting with the 2016 presidential election a number of disturbing instances concerning Mr. Trump's treatment of women came to light," the statement reads. "Similar to how certain members of the entertainment community have been removed from the Academy of Motion Pictures, due to their actions toward women, reflecting a stance on their values by the Academy, this is an opportunity for decision-makers to take a stand on their values in support of women and against disturbing treatment of women. It should be noted that Mr. Trump's star on the Walk of Fame has been destroyed in the past, and has been replaced by the City of Los Angeles using taxpayer funds."

Goodness. It's a good thing the mayor of West Hollywood does not have a star. He has been accused of sexual harassment by a former lover turned staffer, making sexually provocative statements to other City Hall employees and making derogatory comments about women.

In response to West Hollywood's request, the Hollywood Chamber of Commerce said they would review the resolution. But the chamber's president, Leon Gubler, issued the following statement:

"Once we receive a communication from the City of West Hollywood, it will be referred to our Executive Committee for consideration at their next meeting. As of now, there are no plans to remove any stars from the Hollywood Walk of Fame. The West Hollywood City Council does not have jurisdiction over the Hollywood Walk of Fame."

Out of 2,600-plus stars on Hollywood's famed sidewalks, surely there are candidates more deserving of removal than President Trump's.

There are the obvious ones. Bill Cosby stands convicted of sexual assault, and is accused by 60 women of rape and sexual abuse. And, ironically, right next to Trump's star is the star of Kevin Spacey, who has been accused of statutory rape, serial sexual harassment and abuse.

There is Gig Young, the winner of an Academy Award for best supporting actor for the movie "They Shoot Horses, Don't They?" He murdered his fifth wife before turning the gun on himself. The star remains unblemished.

There is bandleader Spade Cooley, who has the distinction of being the only star on the Walk of Fame to be convicted of murder. He beat, stomped and choked his wife to death.

There's Brett Ratner, accused by several women of serial sexual harassment, sexual assault and rape.

The Beatles' John Lennon admitted to physically abusing and hitting women.

Joan Crawford, according to her daughter's autobiography, was a monstrous mother who physically and emotionally abused her adopted child.

Michael Jackson was surrounded by controversy all his life, often spurred by his peculiar tastes, friendships and behavior. Accusations against him ranged from child endangerment for bizarrely dangling his son, Blanket, over a balcony railing, to standing trial on child molestation charges.

Roscoe "Fatty" Arbuckle was accused of raping and accidently killing an actress, who fell ill at a party he hosted and died four days later.

Arnold Schwarzenegger apologized for the instances of sexual harassment that he admittedly engaged in, including unwanted groping and fondling.

Oliver Stone claimed that because of "Jewish domination of the media" the Holocaust is over-represented in films and on TV, and he described Jews as "the most powerful lobby in Washington." He also defended Adolf Hitler as "an easy scapegoat throughout history and it's been used cheaply. He's the product of a series of actions."

Jerry Lee Lewis married his first cousin's daughter when he was 22 and she was 13 years old. The third of his seven wives, he reportedly abused her both physically and emotionally.

Wesley Snipes was found guilty of tax evasion for failing to pay taxes for three years and owed the IRS about $7 million. He served two and a half years in prison, plus a few months under house arrest.

Don Cornelius was arrested on a felony domestic violence charge for spousal abuse against his estranged wife. He originally pleaded not guilty, but later changed his plea to no contest.

John Drew Barrymore had a long history of drug and alcohol abuse, serving jail time for both. Long estranged from his family, he faced charges of abuse and violence, including domestic violence.

They're going to run out of pickaxes.

Trump Haters and Their Double Standards

August 23, 2018

When President Donald Trump revoked the security clearance of former CIA head John Brennan, more than a dozen former high-level intelligence officials fired off a letter that said the President's decision was "ill-considered," "inappropriate" and "deeply regrettable."

The next day, 60 former lower-level CIA officials signed an open letter condemning the act. Their letter read, in part: "All of us believe it is critical to protect classified information from unauthorized disclosure. But we believe equally strongly that former government officials have the right to express their unclassified views on what they see as critical national security issues without fear of being punished for doing so." About a hundred other former officials have since added their names to this letter.

Where were all these officials, so concerned about "critical national security issues," when much of the country—then and now—believed President George W. Bush misled the nation about the Iraq war and the assumption that Saddam Hussein possessed stockpiles of weapons of mass destruction? Ron Fournier, then the Associated Press Washington, D.C. bureau chief, publicly said, "George W. Bush lied us into war in Iraq." To this day, a majority of Democrats, according to several polls, still believe that the entry into the Iraq war was based upon a lie.

Where was the intelligence community's joint letter reminding the country that Bush relied on the unanimous opinion of *all* 16 of our intelligence agencies? Why didn't the intelligence community publish a joint letter defending the integrity of the intelligence community and remind the nation that Bush retained the same CIA director, George Tenet, who served under President Bill Clinton, and said that the assumption that Saddam possessed stockpiles of WMD was a "slam dunk"? But President Trump yanks the security clearance of an ex-CIA director who calls Trump "treasonous"—ie. eligible for the death penalty—and much of the intelligence community throws a hissy fit.

The anti-Trump double standards continue.

The New York Times, for its editorial board, recently hired a tech writer named Sarah Jeong, who in recent years posted anti-white, anti-male and anti-cop messages on Twitter. The New York Times defended the decision by saying Jeong was, in effect, being sarcastic with her caustic posts, simply imitating the hateful nature of her Twitter critics. Call it a form of satire, insisted the Times. But Twitter never banned her, despite her anti-white, anti-cop and anti-male posts.

Conservative pundit Candace Owens tried an experiment. Owens repeated Jeong's posts—except she replaced the word "white" with either "black" or "Jewish." Owens, for example tweeted: "Jewish people are bull---t ... like dogs p---ing on fire hydrants. ... Are Jewish people genetically predisposed to burn faster in the sun?" "Black people are only fit to live underground like groveling goblins." As Owens anticipated, Twitter promptly suspended her account.

Here's another double standard.

President Obama, on several occasions, compared slaves to immigrants. It generated no controversy. But when Trump cabinet member Ben Carson said the same thing, the reaction could not have been more different. At a 2015 naturalization ceremony for new citizens, Obama said: "It wasn't always easy for new immigrants. Certainly it wasn't easy for those of African heritage who had not come here voluntarily, and yet in their own way were immigrants themselves. There was discrimination and hardship and poverty. But, like you, they no doubt found inspiration in all those who had come before them. And they were able to muster faith that, here in America, they might build a better life and give their children something more." Obama, during his presidency, almost a dozen times compared slaves to immigrants whether they "arrived on the Mayflower or on a slave ship, whether they came through Ellis Island or crossed the Rio Grande." His remarks were often received with applause.

Carson said the same thing last year in a speech before HUD employees. "That's what America is about," Carson said, "a land of dreams and opportunity. There were other immigrants who came here in the bottom of slave ships, worked even longer, even harder, for less. But they, too, had a dream that one day their sons, daughters, grandsons, granddaughters, great-grandsons, great-granddaughters, might pursue prosperity and happiness in this land."

Rep. Keith Ellison, D-Minn., insisted that Carson's "slave equals immigrant" perspective means he is unqualified to lead HUD. Carson, said Ellison, "doesn't know how urgent it is to confront racism" in housing. "It's disturbing to me, and it should be to every American, not just black Americans. ... For him, the HUD secretary, to have a stunning misunderstanding of history like that, is really, really striking."

Talk show host Whoopi Goldberg said: "Were the slaves really thinking about the American dream? No, because they were thinking, 'What the hell just happened?!' You know, when people immigrate, they come with the idea that they're going someplace for a better life. ... It's voluntary. ... How does he miss what slavery is?! How does he miss that no slave came to this country willingly? ... Ben, 'Roots.' Watch 'Roots.'"

To be a Trump-hater in good standing, one must employ double standards, hypocrisy and selective outrage. The line forms to the left.

Why Do Ex-Clinton Attack Dogs Davis and Stephanopoulos Get a Pass?

August 30, 2018

Lanny Davis represents Michael Cohen, the lawyer who secretly taped his then-client, now-President Donald Trump.

If you're keeping score, Davis is the same defense lawyer who represented President Bill Clinton during the investigation by special prosecutor Kenneth Starr. To defend Clinton, Davis employed what at the time seemed audacious: a grab-him-by-the-throat-and-rip-his-head-off strategy to vilify Starr. Starr's poll numbers dropped. Davis later admitted, "Whenever I went off the facts and into attacks on Starr, I felt very uncomfortable."

To defend his current client, Davis went on television and said that Cohen has the goods on Trump and can prove Trump directed him to break campaign finance law to pay off Stormy Daniels. Or something like that. Davis' interviewer? George Stephanopoulos.

Yes, this would be the same Stephanopoulos, now ABC News' "chief news anchor," who worked as communications director during the Bill Clinton presidential campaign and as Clinton's senior adviser in the White House. Stephanopoulos *worked with Davis* to employ the aforementioned scorched-earth, attack-Starr strategy. Shouldn't there have been some sort of disclosure by ABC?

But, hey, today's today. Davis insists he only wants "the truth" to come out about Trump's misdeeds. Davis then went on a one-day whirlwind tour of every news and broadcast network where he pitched a crowdfunding campaign to help pay Cohen's legal bills. The "truth" may set you free, but it is not delivered for free.

Watching Davis and Stephanopoulos discuss the Trump/Cohen/Robert Mueller affair was surreal. These men, while defending Clinton 20 years earlier against an investigation they thought illegitimate and charges they thought bogus, designed the very strategy Trump is employing that Davis and Stephanopoulos now decry. Trump is simply following it, only with far more legitimate reasons to question rationale for the investigation and the goals and biases of some of the investigators and lawyers involved.

In June 1998,Tucker Carlson described the way Davis, Stephanopoulos and others "trashed" Starr to defend Clinton. Carlson wrote: "(Clinton campaign chairman James) Carville may have been the first Clinton partisan to attack the independent counsel publicly, but it's clear that the anti-Starr propaganda machine had been under construction for some time. As early as 1995, says former Clinton confidant Dick Morris, George Stephanopoulos and other administration strategists were devising ways to discredit Starr."

Today, Davis and Stephanopoulos just want "truth."

Remember, the Mueller investigation started with a search to determine whether Trump illegally colluded with the Russians to interfere with the 2016 presidential election. Will Stephanopoulos tell his viewers about a story uncovered by the Conservative Review's Jordan Schachtel and One America News Network correspondent Jack Posobiec? Based on their research, BizPac Review reported in a headline, "Lanny Davis Reportedly Making Bank as a Registered Foreign Agent for Putin-Tied Oligarch." The law firm Davis co-founded, Davis Goldberg & Galper, according to Schachtel, "is a registered ACTIVE foreign agent for Ukrainian oligarch Dmytro Firtash, who is a close ally of Russian pres Vladimir Putin." Schachtel also said Foreign Agents Registration Act documents "show Lanny Davis personally lobbied for Firtash."

One more thing about Davis, Cohen and the infamous dossier. Law professor Paul Butler recently claimed on MSNBC: "The Steele dossier keeps getting corroborated by Mueller and reporters. It says that there were two go betweens, the Trump campaign and Russia. The first one was Paul Manafort, and when Manafort resigned from the campaign, Michael Cohen took it over. So we know Manafort is now just chilling, waiting to get through the second trial so he can get his pardon from Trump. So Cohen is the man, if you believe the dossier." Exactly, if you believe the dossier that Butler just insisted "keeps getting corroborated." Except it isn't.

On another show, Davis said that Cohen was "never, never in Prague," and added, "the dossier, so-called, mentions his name 14 times, one of which is a meeting with Russians in Prague. Fourteen times false."

Twenty years ago, Clinton defenders Davis and Stephanopoulos claimed the President's lies about sex were inconsequential. Gloria Allred called his denial and later admission under oath a "sex lie."

So we've gone from collusion to an investigation on payments to a porn star and a Playboy model. So Trump, an ex-playboy with a flashy lifestyle, who spent $66 million of his own money on the campaign, directed his lawyer to break campaign laws to conceal a payment of $130,000. Whatever one thinks about these alleged affairs, they were consensual. Respected liberal writer Christopher Hitchens wrote a book in 1999, called "No One Left to Lie To," about the Bill Clinton impeachment. Hitchens writes about "believable accusations of rape and molestation" including three cases he knew of where Clinton had been accused of rape. One might have thought such accusations would have aroused the media's curiosity even more than alleged voluntary payments for alleged voluntary affairs.

Maybe some reporter will ask ABC's "chief news anchor" the following question: Do rumors of rape by your ex-boss warrant at least as much curiosity as Trump's so-called hush money about alleged consensual affairs?

Aretha's Funeral: Anti-Trump Bigots Hear Truth About the No. 1 Problem in the Black Community

September 6, 2018

President Donald Trump took a pounding at the services for Aretha Franklin. The Rev. Al Sharpton took Trump to task for supposedly demonstrating a lack of respect by saying, "She worked for me on numerous occasions." Other speakers took shots at the President either by name or by implication for his supposed racism and bigotry.

Onstage, in the front row, sat Sharpton, Nation of Islam Minister Louis Farrakhan, the Rev. Jesse Jackson and former President Bill Clinton, all of whom know a thing or two about racism and bigotry. Their careers depend on exaggerating the extent and the impact of anti-black white racism.

At a rally in Harlem in 1991, Sharpton said, "If the Jews want to get it on, tell them to pin their yarmulkes back and come over to my house." A few days later, a young black boy was accidently killed when struck by a car driven by a Hasidic Jew. For three nights, Jews in Crown Heights were subjected to what one Columbia University professor called "a modern-day pogrom" in which two people died and almost 200 were injured. On day two of the riots, Sharpton led a march of about 400 protestors in Crown Heights, shouting, "No justice, no peace." Days later, Sharpton referred derisively to Jews living in Crown Heights as "diamond merchants." A few years later, Sharpton called whites moving businesses into Harlem "interlopers."

Sitting next to Sharpton at Franklin's funeral was Farrakhan, whose hand Clinton shook. As recently as February 2018, Farrakhan said: "Jews were responsible for all of this filth and degenerate behavior that Hollywood is putting out, turning men into women and women into men. White folks are going down. And Satan is going down. And

Farrakhan, by God's grace, has pulled the cover off of that Satanic Jew, and I'm here to say your time is up. Your world is through."

Sitting on Sharpton's other side was Jackson. In 1984, in what Jackson thought was an off-the-record conversation, he referred to Jews as "Hymies" and New York City as "Hymietown." A Washington Post reporter, Milton Coleman, reported Jackson's use of the slur. At first, Jackson denied it. Farrakhan threatened Coleman—a black man—by saying, "If you harm this brother, I warn you in the name of Allah this will be the last one you harm."

This brings us to Clinton, who sat next to Jackson. Clinton, according to "Game Change," the well-received book about the 2008 presidential campaign, contacted Sen. Ted Kennedy to seek his support for Hillary Clinton's candidacy. "A few years ago, this guy would have been getting us coffee," Clinton said of then-presidential candidate Barack Obama. Offended, Kennedy told a friend about what he considered Clinton's racist put-down.

These four onstage—Farrakhan, Sharpton, Jackson and Clinton—have earned a nice living promoting the bogus anti-black-white-racism-remains-a-serious-problem narrative. But at the funeral, one pastor dared to point to the elephant in the room.

The Rev. Jasper Williams Jr. of Salem Bible Church in Atlanta said in his eulogy: "Where is your soul, black man? As I look in your house, there are no fathers in the home no more." He said children need both a "provider" and a "nurturer." He criticized the Black Lives Matter movement: "It amazes me how it is when the police kills one of us we're ready to protest, march, destroy innocent property. We're ready to loot, steal whatever we want, but when we kill 100 of us, nobody says anything; nobody does anything. Black-on-black crime, we're all doing time. We're locked up in our mind. There's got to be a better way. We must stop this today."

The pastor, who decades earlier gave a eulogy for Aretha Franklin's father, got hammered for choosing such a time and place for this "put-down." Even members of the Franklin family rebuked Williams. It is one thing to turn the memorial into a Trump-bashing festival, but a sermon that includes an admonition about accepting personal responsibility, well, that tears it.

Pastor Williams later defended himself, saying, "I'm sure much of the negativity is due to the fact that they don't understand what I'm talking about." He means that many are unaware that almost 70 percent of black kids today are brought into the world by a mother and father who aren't married. That is about 33 percent higher than the percentage of Hispanics and almost 2 1/2 times the percentage of whites.

Williams said: "Anybody who thinks black America is all right as we are now is crazy. We're not all right. It's a lot of change that needs to occur. This change must come from within us. Nobody can give us things to eliminate where we are. We have to change from within ourselves."

Excellent advice. Perhaps Messrs. Sharpton, Farrakhan, Jackson and Clinton were listening.

Nike Pays Kaepernick to Push Peddle False, Harmful Narrative of Police Brutality

September 13, 2018

The NFL's Colin Kaepernick, the quarterback who started the phenomenon of NFL players kneeling during the playing of the national anthem, has finally signed a deal. But not to play football.

No NFL team has offered him a contract since he parted ways with the San Francisco 49ers. His new deal is with Nike, which plans to use him for the 30th anniversary of its "Just Do It" campaign. The Nike ad, over an image of Kaepernick, reads: "Believe in something. Even if it means sacrificing everything."

If Nike truly believed one must "believe in something. Even if it means sacrificing everything," why hasn't the socially conscious company dumped longtime client Tiger Woods? He not only pointedly refuses to condemn President Donald Trump but also recently said: "He's the President of the United States. You have to respect the office. No matter who is in the office, you may like, dislike personality or the politics, but we all must respect the office."

How long has Nike been paying Kaepernick for his "activism"? Some have likened him to Rosa Parks, the civil rights icon who refused to move to the back of the bus, helping spark the modern civil rights movement. Oh, please. Ms. Parks didn't get a shoe deal, and she got arrested for the act of defiance. How has Kaepernick "sacrificed everything"? His NFL career was in decline at the time of his protest. His contract was not likely going to be renewed, even without the controversy that now surrounds him. More important, the NFL, unlike the NBA, does not require its players to stand during the national anthem. So the already rich Kaepernick neither risked losing money nor broke any rule by kneeling.

Remember, the protest began as a criticism of the alleged widespread institutional racism by cops. Kaepernick said, "There are bodies in the street and people getting paid leave and getting away with murder." Actually, the data say otherwise. The Washington Post Fatal Force database reports that 19 unarmed blacks were killed by the police in 2016. Almost 8,000 blacks were homicide victims in 2016, and most died at the hands of another black. Unarmed does not mean not dangerous. Ferguson's Michael Brown was unarmed, but his DNA was found on the police officer's gun, indicating that Brown was trying to grab the gun.

Two studies in recent years found that police are *more reluctant and more hesitant* to use deadly force against a black suspect than a white suspect. Harvard's Roland Fryer, a black economist and the author of one of the studies, said, "It is the most surprising result of my career."

The notion that the police engage in systemic racial profiling is not just wrong—it gets people killed. Because of fears of false allegations of police misconduct, cops in Chicago, according the Mayor Rahm Emanuel, have put themselves in a "fetal" position and do not engage in proactive policing. Why fight crime aggressively if it increases interaction with suspects and therefore increases the chance of a false charge of racism against an officer?

In Baltimore in 2015, an unarmed black man named Freddie Gray died in a police van while being transported to jail. Six officers, including three blacks, were indicted, with charges ranging from second-degree murder for one, to involuntary manslaughter and assault for the others. At the time of Gray's death, the police department was led by a black man. The second in command was also black. The mayor was black. The majority of the Baltimore City Council was black, as was the state attorney who brought the charges. At the time, the U.S. attorney general was black, as was the President of the United States. Three of the cases were tried before a black judge without a jury. The judge found the officers not guilty. And still protestors cried "institutional racism," even though blacks in Baltimore are running the institution.

Trump made the NFL's kneeling protestors a deal that one would have thought could not be refused: "I am gonna ask all of those people to recommend to me ... people that they think were unfairly treated by the justice system ... and I'm gonna take a look at those applications.

And if I find and my committee finds that they were unfairly treated, then we will pardon them, or at least let them out. ... If the players, if the athletes have friends of theirs or people that they know about that have been unfairly treated by the system, let me know."

Where are the names?

Given that the protestors claim there is "structural and systemic racism" and the government runs a "school-to-prison pipeline," they surely can generate an exhaustive list of names. If whites were to spend as much time thinking about how to oppress blacks as Kaepernick thinks they do, they would never have enough time to oppress blacks.

As for Nike, it believes in pursuing its fiduciary obligation—to make profits. It sees no conflict between representing a Woods who refuses to criticize Trump and a Kaepernick who does. If pushing a false narrative of "institutional systemic and structural racism" sells shoes, #justdoit.

The New York Times' Nikki Haley Smear Vs. The New York Times' G.H.W.B. Smear

September 20, 2018

The New York Times' headline read: "Nikki Haley's View of New York Is Priceless. Her Curtains? $52,701." The headline clearly implied that U.S. Ambassador to the United Nations Haley was a profligate elitist Republican unconcerned about spending taxpayer money. As a result, the reaction was swift and strong.

Rep. Ted Lieu, D-Calif., tweeted: "This is not okay. As a Member of the House Foreign Affairs Committee, I call on @HouseForeign Chairman @RepEdRoyce to hold an oversight hearing on @StateDept spending on @nikkihaley and her deputy."

David Hogg, a student gun control advocate, tweeted: "Dear Nikki Haley, There are starving children in America everyday and you have the audacity to misappropriate thousands of tax dollars for your own lavish lifestyle. Resign immediately."

One small problem—the purchase of the curtains was authorized in 2016 during the Obama administration, and Haley had no role in it, a fact originally disclosed in the article's sixth paragraph:

"A spokesman for Ms. Haley said plans to buy the curtains were made in 2016, during the Obama administration. Ms. Haley had no say in the purchase, he said." Clearly, a lot of readers never reached paragraph six.

The New York Times issued a correction but not an apology. The new headline reads, "State Department Spent $52,701 on Curtains for Residence of U.N. Envoy." The edited article also moved the "plans to buy the curtains were made in 2016" sentences up two paragraphs, from sixth to fourth.

The New York Times did a similar hatchet job on then-President George Herbert Walker Bush. During the 1992 election year, a front-page story depicted a supposedly elitist President, so out of touch with the common people that Bush was unfamiliar with a supermarket checkout scanner. The headline? "Bush Encounters the Supermarket, Amazed."

The article began: "As President Bush travels the country in search of re-election, he seems unable to escape a central problem: This career politician, who has lived the cloistered life of a top Washington bureaucrat for decades, is having trouble presenting himself to the electorate as a man in touch with middle-class life."

The article then described a supposedly clueless President:

"Today, for instance, he emerged from 11 years in Washington's choicest executive mansions to confront the modern supermarket.

"Visiting the exhibition hall of the National Grocers Association convention (in Orlando, Florida), Mr. Bush lingered at the mock-up of a checkout lane. He signed his name on an electronic pad used to detect check forgeries. ...

"Then he grabbed a quart of milk, a light bulb and a bag of candy and ran them over an electronic scanner. The look of wonder flickered across his face again as he saw the item and price registered on the cash register screen.

"'This is for checking out?' asked Mr. Bush. 'I just took a tour through the exhibits here,' he told the grocers later. 'Amazed by some of the technology.'

"Marlin Fitzwater, the White House spokesman, assured reporters that he had seen the President in a grocery store. A year or so ago. In Kennebunkport.

"Some grocery stores began using electronic scanners as early as 1976, and the devices have been in general use in American supermarkets for a decade."

One little problem—no New York Times reporter covered this event. Only one "pool" newspaper journalist was there, a Houston Chronicle reporter who filed a two-paragraph report, which said nothing about a befuddled Bush who had never seen a scanner. In fact, after the Times' scanner story came out, a systems analyst for the National Grocers Association, who showed Bush the scanner, said: "The whole thing is ludicrous. What he was amazed about was the ability of the scanner to take that torn label and reassemble it."

A videotape from a pool videographer surfaced. An Associated Press story a week later said: "Bush had stopped by prearrangement at the NCR exhibit before addressing the grocers. He viewed some other high tech equipment, then walked over to the model checkout stand.

"A videotape shot by a White House press pool shows Bush saying, 'This is the scanner, the newest scanner?'

"'Of course, this looks like a typical scanner you'd see in a grocery store,' Graham replied.

"'Yeah,' said Bush.

"'There's one big difference,' said Graham, lifting off the scanner's top plate to reveal a scale underneath. He weighed and rang up a red apple.

"The exhibitor had Bush put the machine through its paces before he showed off what he called the machine's 'really quite amazing' new feature.

"He had Bush scan a card with a universal product code ripped and jumbled into five pieces. The machine read it and rang up the correct sale.

"'Isn't that something,' the President said."

George H. W. Bush lost his bid for re-election in no small measure to the way the media covered him and the economy. Despite over nearly 18 consecutive months of positive economic growth, most Americans considered the economy in recession—presided over, according to the Times, by an out-of-touch Republican patrician.

(831 words)

Ford, Ramirez and a Woman Named Broaddrick

September 27, 2018

As with the first allegation against Supreme Court nominee Brett Kavanaugh, his second accuser, Deborah Ramirez, levels a claim of sexual abuse supposedly witnessed by others.

As to why this accuser came forward, Ronan Farrow, co-author of the New Yorker piece that broke the story, said: "She came forward because Senate Democrats came looking for this claim. She did not flag this for those Democrats. This came to the attention of people on the Hill independently, and it's really cornered her into an awkward position. That's why she took the time to think about this carefully. She said, point-blank, 'I don't want to ruin anyone's life,' but she feels this is a serious claim. She considers her own memories credible, and she felt it was important that she tell her story before others did without her consent, because so many people on the Hill were looking at this story."

Ramirez claims that Kavanaugh sexually confronted her at Yale. According to the New Yorker: "In her initial conversations with The New Yorker, she was reluctant to characterize Kavanaugh's role in the alleged incident with certainty. After six days of carefully assessing her memories and consulting with her attorney, Ramirez said that she felt confident enough of her recollections to say that she remembers Kavanaugh had exposed himself at a drunken dormitory party, thrust his penis in her face, and caused her to touch it without her consent as she pushed him away. Ramirez is now calling for the F.B.I. to investigate Kavanaugh's role in the incident. 'I would think an F.B.I. investigation would be warranted,' she said."

After six days of "assessing her memories"? What exactly does *that* mean?

She named witnesses. About her allegation and the supposed witnesses, The New York Times wrote dismissively: "The Times had interviewed several dozen people over the past week in an attempt to corroborate her story, and could find no one with firsthand knowledge. Ms. Ramirez herself contacted former Yale classmates asking if they recalled the incident and told some of them that she could not be certain Mr. Kavanaugh was the one who exposed himself."

This brings us to the sexual assault allegation against Kavanaugh made by Dr. Christine Blasey Ford. She named three witnesses: Mark Judge, Patrick J. Smyth and Leland Keyser.

Judge, whom Ford claims was in the room during the alleged assault, put out this statement: "In fact, I have no memory of the alleged incident. Brett Kavanaugh and I were friends in high school but I do not recall the party described in Dr. Ford's letter. More to the point, I never saw Brett act in the manner that Dr. Ford describes."

Smyth, through his attorney, issued the following statement: "I understand that I have been identified by Dr. Christine Blasey Ford as the person she remembers as 'PJ' who supposedly was present at the party she described in her statements to the Washington Post. I am issuing this statement today to make it clear to all involved that I have no knowledge of the party in question; nor do I have any knowledge of the allegations of improper conduct she has leveled against Brett Kavanaugh."

Keyser's attorney issued the following statement: "Simply put, Ms. Keyser does not know Mr. Kavanaugh and she has no recollection of ever being at a party or gathering where he was present, with, or without, Dr. Ford."

So, in summary, Ford and Ramirez claim they were sexually assaulted or abused by Kavanaugh, one in prep school, the other in college. As to the first allegation, Ford admits uncertainty about the year, the house where the attack supposedly took place and how she got to and from the party. She admits she told no one for decades and only recently talked about the attack while undergoing couples therapy a few years ago. The named witness to the attacks, as mentioned, has no recollection of this. As to the second allegation, Ramirez named witnesses, none of whom—so far—has corroborated her story. In court, these allegations would not survive a motion to dismiss, given the accuser's burden of proof and the accused's presumption of innocence. This, of course, is not a court of law.

But when Hillary Clinton calls for an FBI investigation into the Ford allegation, the word "shameless" is inadequate. Clinton, of course, failed to call for an FBI investigation into Juanita Broaddrick's claim that she was raped by Bill Clinton. Broaddrick further claimed that, two weeks after the alleged rape, Hillary Clinton verbally threatened Broaddrick to ensure that whatever happened would remain private. Senate Minority Leader Chuck Schumer, D-N.Y., says "there is no presumption of innocence" for Kavanaugh. Sen. Richard Blumenthal, D-Conn., said, "Kavanaugh has a responsibility to come forward with evidence to rebut" the allegations. Sen. Chris Coons, D-Del., said Kavanaugh "bears the burden of disproving these allegations." Sen. Mazie Hirono, D-Hawaii, said, "Not only do these women need to be heard, they need to be believed."

Broaddrick was unavailable for comment.

'White Male Privilege,' RIP

October 4, 2018

What's the last remaining group in America that can be slandered, smeared, maligned and accused of racism, sexism and homophobia with no proof required? White men.

On election night 2016, CNN's Van Jones attributed Donald Trump's victory to "whitelash." That is, racist whites rose up in fear and anger over a country governed for eight years by a black President and in which whites will soon become a demographic minority.

Never mind that Trump actually got a smaller percentage of the white vote than the presumably less racist Mitt Romney in 2012. Trump also got a larger percentage of black, Hispanic and Asian voters than did Romney. He almost bettered Romney's showing with young voters. Of the nearly 700 counties that voted for Barack Obama in 2008 and 2012, more than 200 voted for Trump. Apparently, racism in those counties must have slipped into remission during the eight Obama years, only to bounce back in full force to vote for Trump.

Look at the pummeling "white males" endure by cable TV hosts and pundits commenting on Judge Brett Kavanaugh's confirmation hearings. How many comments veer into a blanket attack against all white men—an attack that would be called racist if leveled at any other racial group?

Many pundits fretted about the "bad optics" of "a group of all white men" questioning Kavanaugh's accuser. This line of attack so spooked the Republicans they brought in a female sex crimes prosecutor to question Dr. Christine Blasey Ford. Of course, even that move, designed to show sensitivity to sex assault survivors, did not escape criticism. One female host called it condescending to "pedal in a girl" to handle the proceedings.

Rep. Jeff Merkley, D-Ore., said: "It seems like the 11 Republican men are not going in with a desire for any sort of a fair process. If they wanted a fair process ... the Republican 11 would say, 'We want that FBI investigation.' We even did that with Anita Hill back there in 1991. Well, here we are, a generation into the future, and we have a more extreme version of Republican men saying they don't even want any form of fairness in this process."

If Republican white men are, by definition, insensitive to women, why do *Democratic* men get a pass?

Anita Dunn, former White House communications director for President Obama, said, "Clearly there is a culture Kavanaugh is trying to deny." This would be the same Dunn who was interviewed for the book "Confidence Men" by Pulitzer Prize-winning journalist and author Ron Suskind. Dunn is quoted as calling Obama's White House a "hostile workplace." At the time, Dunn was not particularly happy with Democratic men. She said—on tape—that "it actually fit all of the classic legal requirements for a genuinely hostile workplace to women." That bombshell is the equivalent of former Trump Communications Director Hope Hicks calling her ex-boss' administration "hostile to women," but the Obama-loving media mostly ignored Dunn's comments.

When white men are not being vilified for their alleged inherent sexism, they are being vilified for their alleged inherent racism. CNN's white male chief legal analyst, Jeffrey Toobin, attributed Hurricane Maria's death total to Trump's pro-white racism: "Isn't the story that these people who died, apparently thousands of them in Puerto Rico—3,000 as you point out—they're not white people. And they don't count to Donald Trump as much as the deaths of white people. I mean, you hate to say that about someone, but look at his record. Isn't that indicative of who he is and what he stands for?"

Meanwhile, at ABC, white George Stephanopoulos, the former Bill Clinton aide who help malign then-President Clinton's accusers, has clearly recovered from any lingering guilt. Discussing the Kavanaugh accusations with Stephanopoulos, White House Press Secretary Sarah Sanders said that "a number of other Democrats should have the same type of scrutiny." Incredibly, given his own history under Clinton, Stephanopoulos responded, "Every single time, the President has taken the side of the man against the women accusers." Sanders demonstrated remarkable restraint in not bringing up Stephanopoulos' astonishing hypocrisy.

White men, you know, are not all bad. Here's a short list: the white Founding Fathers; the white men who fought and died in the war that ended slavery; the white men who fought and died in WWI, WWII, Vietnam, Korea, Afghanistan, Iraq; and the all-white male Supreme Court justices who unanimously decided Brown v. Board of Education.

Many of the Democrats who talk about the racism and sexism of "old white men" are, themselves, old white men. How ironic that white men of the '60s youth movement that pushed for civil rights and racial equality are now considered "racist, sexist, homophobic old white men." That '60s hippie generation insisted, "Never trust anyone over 30." Looks like the lesson was learned only too well.

Lefties of today despise "old white men." But they love their taxes.

If Kavanaugh Is 'Partisan,' Should We Impeach Justice RBG?

October 11, 2018

Forcefully responding to allegations of sex assault, Judge Brett Kavanaugh said in his confirmation hearing rebuttal, "This whole two-week effort has been a calculated and orchestrated political hit—fueled with apparent pent-up anger about President Trump and the 2016 election, fear that has been unfairly stoked about my judicial record, revenge on behalf of the Clintons and millions of dollars in money from outside left-wing opposition groups."

This set off a brand-new argument against Kavanaugh, as his foes began proclaiming that he lacked the appropriate "judicial temperament" to join the Supreme Court.

Apparently, during the last 12 years as a judge on the country's second-most important court, Kavanaugh's judicial temperament was never a problem. Liberal pundits professed "shock" at Kavanaugh's "angry outburst." Is there something called, "The Playbook on Proper Demeanor When Accused Without Corroboration of Attempted Rape"? At stake was not just Kavanaugh's confirmation to the Supreme Court, but his entire livelihood. If, due to uncorroborated allegations of sexual assault, he had lost the confirmation, how could someone so tainted go back to work Monday morning as an appellate judge of the D.C. circuit court?

Retired Supreme Court Justice John Paul Stevens said: "I've changed my views (on Kavanaugh) for reasons that have no really relationship to his intellectual ability or his record as a federal judge. He's a fine federal judge. ... I think that his performance during the hearings caused me to change my mind. ... He has demonstrated a potential bias involving enough potential litigants before the court that he would not be able to perform his full responsibilities, and I think there's merit in that criticism. ... It's not healthy to get a new justice that can only do a part-time job. ... There are enough people who've been put in categories for which he would be unable to sit as a judge."

Approximately 2,400 law professors signed a letter, published in The New York Times, which argued that Kavanaugh's "intemperate, inflammatory and partial manner" rendered him unsuitable to become a Supreme Court justice. The professors said: "We have differing views about the other qualifications of Judge Kavanaugh. But we are united, as professors of law and scholars of judicial institutions, in believing that he did not display the impartiality and judicial temperament requisite to sit on the highest court of our land."

As to what Kavanaugh's so-called conspiratorial view says about his fitness for public service, does this concern extend to presidential candidates? Consider this infamous conspiratorial accusation: "The great story here, for anybody willing to find it and write about it and explain it," then-first lady Hillary Clinton said in 1998, "is this vast right-wing conspiracy that has been conspiring against my husband since the day he announced for president." As a presidential candidate in 2015, Clinton said, "The NRA's position reminds me of negotiating with the Iranians or the communists." To Democrats, Clinton's "conspiratorial world view" did not render her unacceptable as president.

To those who say Kavanaugh disqualified himself as an "impartial jurist," consider the "judicial temperament" of Supreme Court Justice Ruth Bader Ginsburg, a heroic figure to the left. In a July 2016 interview with The New York Times, Ginsburg said of candidate Donald Trump: "I can't imagine what the country would be with Donald Trump as our president" and that her late husband would have said it was "time for us to move to New Zealand."

Undaunted, Ginsburg later told CNN she considered Trump a "faker," adding: "He has no consistency about him. He says whatever comes into his head at the moment. He really has an ego. ... How has he gotten away with not turning over his tax returns? The press seems to be very gentle with him on that."

How's that for bias, judicial temperament and a blatant disregard for the expectation of impartiality? Ginsburg later apologized: "On reflection, my recent remarks in response to press inquiries were ill-advised, and I regret making them. Judges should avoid commenting on a candidate for public office. In the future, I will be more circumspect."

Kavanaugh apologized, too. In an opinion piece published in the Wall Street Journal days before his confirmation, Kavanaugh writes: "At times, my testimony—both in my opening statement and in response to questions—reflected my overwhelming frustration at being wrongly accused, without corroboration, of horrible conduct completely contrary to my record and character. My statement and answers also reflected my deep distress at the unfairness of how this allegation has been handled.

"I was very emotional last Thursday, more so than I have ever been. I might have been too emotional at times. I know that my tone was sharp, and I said a few things I should not have said. I hope everyone can understand that I was there as a son, husband and dad. I testified with five people foremost in my mind: my mom, my dad, my wife, and most of all my daughters."

Liberals see no basis for Ginsburg to recuse herself from cases involving Trump, despite her partisan attack. Will they extend Kavanaugh the same courtesy?

Chris Matthews' Reaction to Kanye West Exposes the Left's Race-Card Hustle

October 18, 2018

As is often the case in this era of President Donald Trump, the reaction is far more interesting than the action.

The action was rapper/entrepreneur, ex-George W. Bush denouncer and Trump supporter Kanye West, whom Trump invited to the White House. The reaction from left-wing black critics was predictable. But the reaction from a notable Trump-hating white pundit was unintentionally eye-opening. In the Oval Office, West spoke nonstop, and apparently unscripted, for nearly 10 minutes. During his monologue and subsequent questions by reporters, West talked about the pressure blacks face to vote Democratic; how conservative blacks are often bullied by other blacks into supporting the Democratic Party; and how the Second Amendment is unrelated to gun violence, because "illegal guns is the problem, not legal guns." But most importantly, he spoke about the pain he experienced growing up without a father.

First, the reaction by black critics. Last month, rapper Snoop Dogg called West an "Uncle Tom"—and that was before West's visit to the White House. After West's Oval Office monologue, rapper T.I. called him a "Sambo." On CNN, Bakari Sellers, a Democratic strategist, said, "Kanye West is what happens when Negroes don't read." CNN "political commentator" Tara Setmayer called West a "token Negro" and described him as "an attention whore, like the President." Apparently, Setmayer forgot about the numerous celebrities, including rappers, who visited President Barack Obama during his eight years in the White House.

How dare West point to the most important issue, by far, in the black community: the number of children growing up in homes without fathers! After all, Obama, who also grew up without his biological father, even said, "Children who grow up without a father are five times more likely to live in poverty and commit crime, nine times more likely to drop out of school and 20 times more likely to end up in prison."

The late rapper Tupac Shakur, who also grew up without a father, said: "I know for a fact that had I had a father, I'd have some discipline. I'd have more confidence. ... Your mother cannot calm you down the way a man can. Your mother can't reassure you the way a man can. ... You need a man to teach you how to be a man."

Then-Sen. Obama said the same thing in 2008: "I know the toll it took on me, not having a father in the house—the hole in your heart when you don't have a male figure in the home."

In regard to West being called a "coon," a "sell-out," "self-loathing" and an "Uncle Tom," Obama also knows a thing or two about that. In 2000, when he ran for Congress against Rep. Bobby Rush, D-Ill., Rush branded Obama as an out-of-touch, not-from-the-'hood, Harvard-educated elite who taught at University of Chicago and who was not "truly black." Then-state Sen. Obama, beaten badly in the race, said, "When Congressman Rush and his allies attack me for going to Harvard and teaching at the University of Chicago, they're sending a signal to black kids that if you're well-educated, somehow you're not 'keeping it real.'" As President, Obama later said: "There's no one way to be black. Take it from somebody who's seen both sides of debate about whether I'm black enough."

Second, let's examine the reaction to West's White House visit from a prominent Trump-hating white critic, MSNBC's Chris Matthews. Analyzing why Trump invited Kanye West to the White House, Matthews inadvertently exposed the liberals' game of using the race card for votes. Matthews said the main reason Trump invited West was to assuage white voters' concerns about Trump. Matthews said, "White people won't vote for a guy—most of them—if they think they're racist."

Hold on!

Most nights, Matthews and his left-wing cable colleagues scramble to come up with new and different ways to call Trump "racist." They argue that Trump knowingly and intentionally crafts his message to appeal to white racists. On election night, CNN's Van Jones attributed

Trump's victory to "whitelash"—claiming that "racist" white voters found a kindred spirit in "racist" Donald Trump. But Matthews, in an unguarded moment, conceded that most whites would not vote for somebody if they thought he or she was racist.

The con has been exposed.

Matthews said, in effect, that most white people are not racist, would not vote for a racist and therefore only a brain-dead white politician would run an election catering to racists. Yet virtually every night, he and his guests preach racism, racism, racism in America.

In fact, Matthews echoes the words of John O'Sullivan, then-editor of the National Review. Sullivan, in 1997, said, "White racism does exist, but its social power is weak and the social power arrayed against it overwhelming."

To the left, the only acceptable blacks are victicrats who believe racism is the top problem. Never mind the liberals—like Obama—who know damn well the top problem is fatherlessness. But Democratic politicians—like Obama—also need to keep blacks angry for votes.

Quite the Faustian bargain.

The 'Voter ID Is Racist' Con

October 25, 2018

Add late-night comic Trevor Noah to the list of ill-informed lefties who consider voter identification a "racist" demand intended to "suppress" the black vote.

"Isn't it interesting," Noah said, "how every time Republicans create a voting restriction, it just so happens to disproportionately affect people of the brown-brown? ... Let's be honest, you don't have to say who you're targeting to target someone. You just have to know which rules are likely to hit them the most."

Noah echoes the sentiment of then-Attorney General Eric Holder, who in 2014 characterized the call for voter ID laws as an example of "pernicious" racism. Last week, MSNBC's Chris Matthews told Holder's successor, former Attorney General Loretta Lynch, that Republicans push voter ID laws to "screw the African-American voter." Lynch responded: "Yes, yes—and it's nothing new. ... This is a historical issue. It's a current issue. And it's only history because it happened to somebody else, not because it could never happen again. That's what's happening now."

Former Vice President Joe Biden called Trump's assertion that millions of people voted illegally in the 2016 election a "flat lie." But Biden did not stop there. The Republican support for voter ID, he said, was all about suppressing minority votes: "It's what these guys are all about, man. Republicans don't want working-class people voting. They don't want black folks voting." Last year, Sen. Elizabeth Warren, D-Mass., denounced "racist voter ID laws and voter suppression tactics (that) sprout like weeds all across the country." In a press conference in July, CNN's April Ryan asked White House Press Secretary Sarah Sanders: "So, Sarah, since you keep saying that the President is very concerned about the election process ... you did not mention voter suppression in that. Voter suppression has been an issue for decades and particularly in these last few elections."

Despite these alleged racist roadblocks to the ballot box, in 2008 blacks voted at a higher percentage than whites. That same year, liberal Supreme Court Justice John Paul Stevens wrote one of the majority opinions in a 6-3 case that upheld Indiana's voter ID law, which required voters to show a photo ID—such as a driver's license or passport—before casting their votes. Stevens recognized "flagrant examples of (voter) fraud" throughout America's history and wrote that "not only is the risk of voter fraud real" but "it could affect the outcome of a close election." The additional burden on voters, Stevens argued, is more than offset by "the state's interest in counting only the votes of eligible voters."

Blacks also support voter ID. A 2016 Gallup poll found that 77 percent of non-whites support voter ID, nearly as high as the 81 percent of whites who support it.

The fact that voter ID is legal and popular does not, of course, affect the view that it "suppresses" the minority vote. The George Soros-supported website ThinkProgress ran a story last year with this menacing headline: "New Study Confirms that Voter ID Laws Are Very Racist."

Citing research by three professors from U.C. San Diego, Michigan State and Bucknell University, the article says: "turnout among Hispanic voters is '7.1 percentage points lower in general elections and 5.3 points lower in primaries' in states with strict voter ID laws. The laws also reduce turnout among African-American and Asian-American voters. White turnout, according to their study, is 'largely unaffected.'"

Case closed? Not exactly.

A follow-up study by researchers from Yale, Stanford and the University of Pennsylvania found no evidence that voter ID laws have a statistically significant impact on voter turnout. This study examined the methodology and conclusions of the previous study. Its researchers wrote: "Widespread concern that voter identification laws suppress turnout among racial and ethnic minorities has made empirical evaluations of these laws crucial. But problems with administrative records and survey data impede such evaluations. ... We show that the results of the paper are a product of data inaccuracies (and) the presented evidence does not support the stated conclusion ... When errors are corrected, one can recover positive, negative or null estimates of the effect of voter ID laws on turnout, precluding firm conclusions."

In other words, the data do not support the notion that the "brown-brown" are too dumb, too lazy or otherwise incapable of obtaining the necessary identification to vote.

Pittsburgh Synagogue Massacre: Obama Slams 'Hateful Rhetoric'—Did He Mean Trump's, or His Own?

November 1, 2018

Former President Barack Obama received praise for his response to the recent murder of 11 people at a Pittsburgh synagogue. Obama tweeted: "We grieve for the Americans murdered in Pittsburgh. All of us have to fight the rise of anti-Semitism and hateful rhetoric against those who look, love, or pray differently." Many described Obama's words as a powerful call for "unity."

Meanwhile, leaders of Bend the Arc, a Pittsburgh Jewish advocacy group, said President Donald Trump is *not* welcome in their city until Trump "denounces white nationalism"—the white supremacist movement that many believe Trump is guilty of either supporting or at least providing aid and comfort.

Speaking of "hateful rhetoric," critics of President Trump have apparently forgotten about Obama's 20-year relationship with his anti-Semitic pastor, the Rev. Jeremiah Wright. After 9/11, Wright called the attacks retribution, in part, for America's support of Israel. In a 2009 interview, Wright said: "Them Jews ain't going to let (Obama) talk to me. ... They will not let him to talk to somebody who calls a spade what it is. ... Ethnic cleansing is going on in Gaza. Ethnic cleansing (by) the Zionist is a sin and a crime against humanity, and they don't want Barack talking like that because that's anti-Israel."

Wright and Nation of Islam Minister Louis Farrakhan have long been friends. In 2007, the publication founded by Wright's church, Trumpet Newsmagazine, awarded its annual "Dr. Jeremiah A. Wright Jr. Trumpeter Award" to Farrakhan, a man who, it said, "truly epitomized greatness." Farrakhan, in a February 2018 sermon, proclaimed the era of

Jewish influence was near its end. Farrakhan said: "White folks are going down. And Satan is going down. And Farrakhan, by God's grace, has pulled the cover off of that Satanic Jew, and I'm here to say your time is up, your world is through." In 2005, Farrakhan posed with a smiling freshman senator named Barack Obama. Fortunately for Obama, the photograph was not released until after Obama completed his two terms in the White House. Long-time Democrat Alan Dershowitz says that had he known about that photograph, he would not have campaigned for Obama.

Obama often denounced cops. Shortly after his election, black Harvard professor Louis Gates—a friend of Obama's—couldn't open his front door upon returning home from a trip. Gates asked his driver for assistance. A neighbor, observing two people trying to force open Gates' front door, called 911. The Cambridge, Massachusetts, cops responded, and politely requested that Gates, now inside the house, step outside and prove he lived there. Rather than cooperate, Gates made flippant comments to the cops, escalating the matter. Obama later said, "The Cambridge police acted stupidly." No, they hadn't.

In Ferguson, Missouri, Michael Brown, an unarmed black man, was killed by a police officer. A friend and witness claimed that Brown held his hands up and pleaded with the cop, "Don't shoot." A grand jury later found the assertion a lie and completely exonerated the officer. But before the investigation was complete, Obama invoked Ferguson during a United Nations address as an example of the systemic racism blacks allegedly face in our criminal justice system.

Obama's Attorney General Eric Holder falsely claimed that due to "pernicious" racism, the "criminal justice system ... treats groups of people differently and punishes them unequally." But the U.S. Sentencing Commission concluded that the longer sentences result from "legitimate factors." The typical black defendant has a longer criminal record than does a white defendant, and during sentencing, judges often consider defendants' criminal records.

President Obama, commenting on the 2016 police shootings of unarmed blacks, said: "These are not isolated incidents. They are symptomatic of a broader set of racial disparities that exist in our criminal justice system." But recent studies, including one done by a black Harvard economist, show the opposite. Cops, the studies found, are *more* hesitant to use deadly force on a black suspect than a white one.

In 2014, two NYPD officers were killed—literally executed—while sitting in their squad cars. In 2016, five Dallas cops and three Baton Rouge, Louisiana, cops were also killed. All three suspects in these cop killings were black men, motivated, according to their own social media postings, by Black Lives Matter's claim of anti-black systemic racism in the criminal justice system.

After the Dallas shootings, William Johnson, the executive director of the National Association of Police Organizations, said, "I think (the Obama administration's) continued appeasement at the federal level with the Department of Justice; their appeasement of violent criminals; their refusal to condemn movements like Black Lives Matter actively calling for the death of police officers ... while blaming police for the problems in this country has led directly to the climate that has made Dallas possible."

Trump's critics argue that his alleged "hateful rhetoric" inspired the pipe bomb suspect and the suspected Pittsburgh synagogue shooter. As for the cops murdered in New York, Baton Rouge and Dallas, does the same logic apply to Obama and his anti-cop rhetoric?

Midterms: Republicans Had a Great Story to Tell—and It Staved Off Disaster

November 8, 2018

As expected, Democrats regained control of the House of Representatives. But the much-anticipated "blue wave" failed to appear. History shows that the first midterm election for the party in the White House usually results in a loss, often a big loss, in that party's House members. President Barack Obama, for example, lost 63 seats in the House and 6 seats in the Senate in the 2010 midterms. In the 21 midterm elections held from 1934 through 2014, the President's party has gained seats in both the Senate and the House only twice: during Franklin Delano Roosevelt's and George W. Bush's first midterm elections. The 2018 GOP House lost seats, more than the 23 seats Democrats needed to flip, but not nearly the thumping the Democrats hoped for.

Forty Republicans—three senators and 37 representatives—chose not to run for re-election in 2018, while another 14 left their offices early or announced their resignations. This hurt. Only 18 Democrats declined to seek re-election, with another four leaving office early or resigning. From 1964 through 2016, 85 to 98 percent of House incumbents seeking re-election won.

In January 2018, NPR ran a story about the record number of House Republicans who decided not to seek re-election. Rep. Charlie Dent, R-Penn., according to NPR's Kelsey Snell, "didn't want to spend the next 10 months talking about or defending President Trump." Dent said: "You know, this campaign cycle, 2018, will simply be a referendum on the President. We'll be talking about him and his latest tweet or comment or an incendiary remark or whatever. So you're really not speaking about or talking about major issues." In short, Trump would be on the ballot in the midterms, and Dent, likely echoing the fears of fellow Republicans who chose not to run, wanted no part in defending Trump.

But on Tuesday, Democrats lost several marquee races where high-power surrogates like Barack Obama, Joe Biden and Oprah Winfrey campaigned. Democrat Beto O'Rourke lost his Texas senate bid to Ted Cruz. Democrat Stacey Abrams appears to have lost the Georgia governor's race. Democrat Andrew Gillum lost the Florida governor race to Republican Ron DeSantis, for whom Trump energetically campaigned. For the most part, where Trump campaigned, his candidate won. That Republicans held off the much anticipated giant blue wave and limited the gubernatorial losses to about a half a dozen reflects the degree to which the media, and many Republicans, still underestimate Trump.

Remember when serious pundits urged electors to refuse to certify Trump's election? Several congressional Democrats refused to attend Trump's inauguration, where the new President gave an address that Democrats and many in the media described as "combative" and "divisive" and "partisan." Some critics even predicted that, because of Trump's alleged "mental instability," a cabinet official or another "adult in the administration" would invoke the 25th Amendment. This drumbeat grew so loud that Trump's White House doctor discussed the results of Trump's physical at a press conference, where reporters asked about Trump's mental fitness to serve. Pundits and cable hosts practically ran out of adjectives while calling Trump "racist," "sexist," "anti-Semitic," "homophobic" and "xenophobic."

When the deputy attorney general appointed Robert Mueller to investigate the allegation of a Trump-Russia "collusion," Trump-haters began the countdown on when they expected Trump to resign, one step before Mueller outed him as an election cheat. Rep. Maxine Waters, D-Calif., called for Trump's impeachment almost from the moment he took office.

When Trump visited Speaker Paul Ryan, Democratic House members not only heckled, but some held up signs critical of Trump and his policy of separating families that tried to enter through our southern border. CNN's Don Lemon has called Trump "racist." According to "nonpartisan" Pew Research Center, 90 percent of broadcast networks' (ABC, CBS and NBC) news coverage of Trump has been negative. With the exception of Fox News, Trump takes a nightly battering on cable news.

But a funny thing happened on the way to this year's midterms. The stock market kept hitting record highs. The majority of Americans, for the first time in years, felt confident about their personal economic condition and future. 2018's first two quarters of GDP growth came in at 2.2 and 4.2 percent, with the third quarter registering a strong 3.5 percent. In October, 250,000 jobs were created, exceeding expectations. Black unemployment reached its the lowest percent since the Bureau of Labor Statistics began tracking unemployment by race in the '70s. An NAACP poll released in August put Trump's approval rate at 21 percent for blacks. The Nov. 5, 2018 Rasmussen daily Presidential Tracking Poll showed Trump with an approval rating 5 points higher than Obama's at the same point in his presidency.

Republicans had a good story to tell, and it staved off disaster. Had fewer GOP House incumbents decided not to run, the results would have been even better for Republicans. Yes, for the next two years, Trump will face investigation after investigation. But for the Republican Party as a whole, Tuesday could have been worse, much worse.

If Trump Is 'Racist,' He Needs to Go Back to Racism School

November 15, 2018

Abraham Lincoln, when informed that General Ulysses S. Grant was a drunk, famously asked Grant's accusers what whiskey he was drinking so Lincoln could send a barrel to every general in the army. Keep this in mind when President Donald Trump's critics accuse him of "racism" against blacks.

Under this "racist" President, black unemployment, since the government began keeping numbers, hit an all-time low in May. Polls show that inner-city parents want choice in education: specifically, they want the means to opt out of sending their children to an under-performing government school the child has been mandated to attend. Think tanks on the left (like the Brookings Institution) and think tanks on the right (like the Heritage Foundation) pretty much agree on the formula to escape poverty: finish high school; get married before having a child; and do not have that child before you are financially capable of assuming that responsibility.

But what about the quality of that high school education? A 2004 Fordham Institute study found that 44 percent of Philadelphia public-school teachers with school-age children of their own placed them in private schools. By 2013, the nationwide average for private-school attendance was 11 percent of white families and 5 percent of black families. Clearly, Philadelphia teachers, on teachers' salaries, make the sacrifice to send their own kids where they have a better chance of success.

About choice in education, Trump's secretary of education, Betsy DeVos, said: "What can be done about (improving primary education) is empowering parents to make the choices for their kids. Any family that has the economic means and the power to make choices is doing so for their children. Families that don't have the power—that can't decide 'I'm gonna move from this apartment in downtown whatever to the suburb, where I think the school is gonna be better for my child'—if they don't have that choice and they are assigned to that school, they are stuck there. I am fighting for the parents who don't have those choices. We need all parents to have those choices."

A 2016 poll in "Education Next" found that 64 percent of blacks supported "a tax credit for individual and corporate donations that pay for scholarships to help low-income parents send their children to private schools." Similarly, A 2015 PDK/Gallup Poll found that 68 percent of blacks wanted the ability to "choose which public schools in the community the students attend, regardless of where they live."

Trump also wants to stop illegal immigration. Why should that matter to urban blacks? Harvard economist George Borjas, in his 2013 research paper "Immigration and the American Worker," wrote: "Classifying workers by education level and age and comparing differences across groups over time shows that a 10 percent increase in the size of an education/age group due to the entry of immigrants (both legal and illegal) reduces the wage of native-born men in that group by 3.7 percent and the wage of all native-born workers by 2.5 percent." As to illegal immigration, Borjas says: "Although the net benefits to natives from illegal immigrants are small, there is a sizable redistribution effect. Illegal immigration reduces the wage of native workers by an estimated $99 to $118 billion a year, and generates a gain for businesses and other users of immigrants of $107 to $128 billion."

But what about how the President "insults black people"? After Trump's recent testy exchange with a black reporter, CNN's Jeffrey Toobin said: "There is a racial dimension to this. The fact that the President is always—the idea that this was some random selection of journalists he doesn't like is not the case. It's always black people with this President." Really?

What race was Robert De Niro when Trump called him "a very low IQ individual"? What race was Rosie O'Donnell when Trump called her "dumb"? What race was MSNBC's Joe Scarborough when Trump called him "crazy"? What race was former Texas Gov. Rick Perry when, during a campaign speech, Trump mocked him for his eyewear? "He put on glasses so people think he's smart. ..." said Trump. "People can see through the glasses." What race was MSNBC's Mika Brzezinski when Trump called her "dumb as a rock"? How many white politicians does Trump slam when he criticizes "stupid" trade deals?

If Trump set out to hurt blacks by pushing economic policies that helped reduce black unemployment to an all-time low; by attempting to stop unskilled illegal alien workers from competing with unskilled blacks for jobs and wages; and by empowering inner-city black parents, rather than the government, to pick the school for their children, then Trump needs to go back to racism school.

Don't Let Trump Hatred Thwart the School Choice Movement

November 22, 2018

The Detroit school board recently voted 6-to-1 to consider removing Dr. Ben Carson's name from one of its high schools. Carson, a former Detroit student and former head of pediatric neurology at Johns Hopkins Hospital, pioneered several groundbreaking neurosurgical procedures. He now serves as President Donald Trump's secretary of housing and urban development. But one school board member said Carson's name on the school is comparable to "having Trump's name on our school in blackface."

About Detroit public schools, Wisconsin Institute for Law & Liberty's C.J. Szafir and Cori Petersen recently wrote, "In 2017 Detroit ranked last in proficiency out of 27 large urban school districts with a measly 5 percent of fourth-graders proficient in math and 7 percent in reading." Maybe the Detroit school board should invest the time they spent inquiring about Carson's reputation in improving its pupils' education.

Let's hope that hatred for Trump does not stall the growing movement for private school choice as an alternative to public K-12 education. A 2015 survey conducted by Knowledge Networks for Education Next found that nationally, 13 percent of non-teacher parents have sent one or more of their school-age kids to private school for at least some of their K-12 schooling. But 20 percent of teachers with children have done the same. The number is much higher for teachers in urban areas.

A 2004 Fordham Institute study found that in Philadelphia, a staggering 44 percent of public-school teachers with school-age kids sent their own children to private schools. In Cincinnati-Hamilton

County and Chicago, 41 and 39 percent of public school teachers, respectively, paid for a private school education for their children. In Rochester, New York, it was 38 percent. In Baltimore, it was 35 percent. San Francisco-Oakland-Vallejo was 34 percent, and New York-Northeastern New Jersey was almost 33 percent. In Los Angeles-Long Beach, nearly 25 percent of public school teachers sent their kids to private school versus 16 percent of all Angelenos who did so.

Hats off to all the hardworking teachers and administrators working in urban schools, which are frequently in and among the worst schools in the worst areas, with often unmotivated students from homes where education is not emphasized. Without an authority figure in the home ensuring that that the child has done his homework and gone to bed on time, the teacher's job becomes exponentially more difficult. And bravo to hard-working parents who want to ensure that their children get a quality education.

Most urban parents support choice in education, despite the opposition of the public education establishment. Polls show about 80 percent of inner-city parents want vouchers, and most careful studies show that private school choice produces better outcomes.

But wait. A recent study from the University of Virginia's highly regarded Curry School of Education found "no evidence that private schools, exclusive of family background or income, are more effective for promoting student success." Hogwash, says Michael Q. McShane, the national research director of EdChoice, a pro-choice advocacy group, who argues that the UVA study lacked "randomization." Under "randomization," McShane says: "Everyone who wants a voucher gets their name thrown in a hopper and random chance is the only thing that differs between those who get a voucher and those who don't. That's how we know that any differences between the two groups can be attributed to the program."

The Wisconsin Institute for Law & Liberty wrote last year: "The Milwaukee Parental Choice Program works. ... Out of 11 gold standard studies on the program, 10 have shown that students in the MPCP outperform their peers at Milwaukee Public Schools (one study showed no significant difference). ... Students in the MPCP outperformed their peers in public schools in both math and reading on the Forward Exam when appropriate 'apples-to-apples' comparisons are made. We also found that MPCP students score about 7.7 percent higher on the ACT than MPS students, a difference that could determine whether a student gets into college or not in some cases."

Thomas Sowell, who supports private school choice, also emphasizes the importance of comparing apples to apples. "My favorite way of making comparisons among truly comparable students," says Sowell, "is to get educational results from schools where both the charter school and the traditional public school are located in the very same building, teaching the same grade levels, and with the students being tested by the very same tests." When examined that way, school choice works.

About Milwaukee, Szafir and Petersen wrote: "Many parents have turned to the Milwaukee Parental Choice Program, passed in 1990, which provides low-income children with vouchers for private schools. Over the past decade, enrollment has increased 45 percent at MPCP schools and by 47 percent at the city's charter schools."

If private school choice does not yield benefit, can someone explain why programs that provide choice consistently have long lines of parents who want to enroll their students? Trump wants to give urban parents an opt-out of an underperforming government school. Resistance against Trump ought not to translate into resistance against parents who want a better future for their children.

On Immigration, Hillary Clinton and John Kerry Discover Their Inner Trump

November 29, 2018

If President Donald Trump were paid a dime every time critics call his anti-illegal immigration policy "racist," he'd double his net worth. Never mind that at one time, President Bill Clinton, former Democratic Senate Leader Harry Reid, former Sen. Barack Obama, D-Ill., and Sen. Dianne Feinstein, D-Calif., all warned about the problems associated with illegal immigration.

Reid, for example, railed against birthright citizenship in 1993: "If making it easy to be an illegal alien isn't enough, how about offering a reward for being an illegal immigrant? No sane country would do that, right? Guess again. If you break our laws by entering this country without permission and give birth to a child, we reward that child with U.S. citizenship." Apart from America, the only other rich, industrial countries that allow birthright citizenship—automatically bestowed at birth—are Canada and Chile. Not a single European country permits this.

As to legal immigration, Trump, too, stands accused of racism for seeking to end "chain migration" and for arguing that legal immigrants must benefit America, rather than the other way around.

But recently, Hillary Clinton, Trump's 2016 presidential rival, and former Secretary of State John Kerry argued that *Europe* should enact more restrictive immigration policies. "I think Europe needs to get a handle on migration because that is what lit the flame," said Clinton last week in an interview with The Guardian, referring to the hot-button issue of immigration among voters. "I admire the very generous and compassionate approaches that were taken by leaders like (Germany's) Angela Merkel, but I think it is fair to say Europe has done its part and must send a very clear message—'we are not going to be able to continue (to) provide refuge and support'—because if we don't deal with the migration issue it will continue to roil the body politic."

Eskinder Negash, the president of the U.S. Committee for Refugees and Immigrants, a migrant rights organization, told The New York Times that he "was kind of shocked" by Clinton's statement. "If she's simply saying you need to cut down on refugees coming to Europe to ask for asylum because they have a well-founded fear of persecution, just to appease some right-wing political leaders, it's just not the right thing to do," said Negash.

Rep. Pramila Jayapal, D-Wash., called Clinton's words a "deeply misguided and unfortunate comment from someone who must know better." Former Clinton adviser Peter Daou tweeted: "Why is #HillaryClinton playing into the hands of right-wing haters? The problem isn't the migrants, it's the xenophobes. I try to avoid politics on #Thanksgiving but this is just wrong." Rolling Stone's Jamil Smith tweeted: "This is a sickening capitulation on her part. You don't stop racism by giving in to racists." New Yorker staff writer Osita Nwanevu tweeted: "Climate change, a crisis created by the developed world, is going to force poor people across the globe to move in order to survive. The approach Clinton is advocating will be a death sentence for millions and millions of people, and we should be clear about that."

In response to the criticism, Clinton blamed Trump. "Trump has made it worse with cruel abuses at the border," tweeted Clinton, "detaining children and separating them from their families. It's one of the most shameful moments in our history." But in her "clarification," she *still* sounded like Trump. "In a recent interview," Clinton tweeted, "I talked about how Europe must reject right-wing nationalism and authoritarianism, including by addressing migration with courage and compassion. ... On both sides of the Atlantic, we need reform. Not open borders, but immigration laws enforced with fairness and respect for human rights. We can't let fear or bias force us to give up the values that have made our democracies both great and good. ... The EU needs a more comprehensive policy that builds societies that are both secure and welcoming."

Kerry, speaking at a recent event in London one week before Clinton's interview, also warned Europe about its immigration policy, which in the last few years has admitted millions of migrants, mostly from the Greater Middle East and Africa. Kerry warned: "Europe's already crushed under this transformation that's taken place because of immigration. Germany—Angela Merkel, weakened because of it. And other places impacted, Italy—significantly impacted its politics by immigration."

Then there's the Dalai Lama. Two years ago, before Trump became the Republican nominee for president, the Dalai Lama said, "There are too many (migrants) now. ... Europe, for example, Germany, cannot become an Arab country. Germany is Germany. ... From a moral point of view, too, I think that refugees should only be admitted temporarily."

The criticism Clinton faced from the left over her practical, commonsensical analysis says a lot about where Democrats stand on immigration—legal and illegal. Much of the Democratic base ignores this issue, is indifferent about it or has done a cost-benefit analysis and believes that immigrants-turned-citizens-turned-mostly-Democrat-voters outweigh the financial, social or political price.

Fake Praise for GHWB: Where Were Media When He Needed Them?

December 6, 2018

As with the passing of former President Ronald Reagan, the media are in full praise mode following the death of former President George Herbert Walker Bush. Where were they when the one-term President needed them? In Reagan's case, even his haters grudgingly acknowledged the overall success of his presidency. As for Bush 41, the media's praise of Bush's "grace" and "class" serves to indirectly to attack President Donald Trump by showing the contrast between the two Republicans' styles and characters.

But what did much of the liberal media think and say about Bush at the time?

When Bush announced his intention to seek the presidency in 1988, a Newsweek cover story showed the former New Englander navigating a small boat—get it, he's elite—with the caption "Fighting the Wimp Factor." Wimp? Bush joined Navy on his 18th birthday, serving in WWII as the Navy's second-youngest aviator. He flew 58 combat missions, was shot down by the Japanese and was rescued by an American sub.

When he ran in 1988, his resume included almost seven years as Reagan's vice president, two terms as a member of the U.S. House of Representatives, director of central intelligence, head of the Republican National Committee, ambassador to the U.N. and de facto ambassador to China, in addition to being a decorated WWII fighter pilot. President Barack Obama was apparently unimpressed: In 2016, he said, "There has never been any man or woman more qualified for this office than Hillary Clinton."

Despite Bush's mind-numbingly impressive credentials, he somehow found himself tagged as insufficiently macho. In 1997, Evan Thomas' Newsweek wrote: "Bush suffers from a potentially crippling handicap—a perception that he isn't strong enough or tough enough for the challenges of the Oval Office. That he is, in a single mean word, a wimp." The year before, Republican pundit George Will called him a "lapdog." A Washington Post editorial now praises Bush. Yet neither the Post nor The New York Times endorsed him for president in 1988 or 1992.

In fact, during his presidency, The New York Times aided and abetted the narrative of an elite "out-of-touch" patrician. During the 1992 election year, the Times ran a front-page story about a President so clueless about the life of the average American that he was unfamiliar with the supermarket checkout scanner. But the story was fake. A National Grocers Association systems analyst, the man who showed Bush the scanner, said: "The whole thing is ludicrous. What he was amazed about was the ability of the scanner to take that torn label and reassemble it."

Black Democrats like Rep. Maxine Waters, D-Calif., called him "racist." In 1992, Waters said: "(Bush) is a mean-spirited man who has no care or concern about what happens to the African-American community in this country. I truly believe that."

Bush stood accused of racism for "using" the infamous Willie Horton ad that ran during the 1988 campaign, even though his campaign had not produced the ad. Furthermore, the issue of his opponent Michael Dukakis' Massachusetts furlough program was first brought up by Dukakis' Democratic rival Al Gore. Under Dukakis' program, Horton, a convicted murderer, committed rape while out on furlough.

Bush, pressured by Democrats and some in his own party, broke the famous pledge he made at the 1988 Republican convention: "Read my lips. No new taxes." NBC News' Andrea Mitchell now says "breaking that pledge showed the character and resolve of the man." Similarly, Newsweek's Thomas now calls the broken tax promise an act of "courage." But asked in a 1992 press conference whether he considered breaking the pledge "the biggest mistake" of his presidency, Bush said, "Well, I don't know about the biggest, but yes ... I'm very disappointed with Congress." At the 1992 Republican convention, he apologized for breaking the pledge. James Carville, Clinton's lead campaign strategist, called it "the most famous broken promise in the history of American politics."

Did reporters reward Bush for his tax concession? Hardly. A poll of Washington, D.C., reporters found that, in 1992, 89 percent of them voted for Bill Clinton. Only 7 percent voted for Bush.

In October 1992, according to Investor's Business Daily, over 90 percent of the economic news in newspapers was negative. At the time, the economy was well into a recovery, on its 19th consecutive month of growth. Yet much of the business news was sour. In November 1992, Bill Clinton won. That month, only 14 percent of the newspapers' economic news was negative. As recently as 2012, a PBS documentary repeatedly insisted Bill Clinton inherited an economy in "recession." In fact, the GDP in Bush's final quarter grew 3.8 percent.

When son George W. Bush won the presidency in 2000, mom Barbara Bush expressed surprise. "You're not going to like this," she said, "but my gut feeling is that all the media is against George, Republicans, any Republican." Indeed. From that very media, currently fawning over a man they now call a "statesman," George Herbert Walker Bush deserved better. Much better.

Mueller Probe: If Convictions Equals Success, Whitewater Was a Triumph

December 13, 2018

President Donald Trump-haters salivated over special counsel Robert Mueller's recent filings on ex-Trump campaign manager Paul Manafort and Trump former lawyer/"fixer" Michael Cohen. In both cases, Mueller recommends lengthy sentences, having accused them of committing crimes, including, in the case of Cohen, that Trump directed him to violate campaign finance laws in paying off porn star Stormy Daniels and Playboy Playmate Karen McDougal.

If true, is an *impeachable* offense?

In 2013, the Federal Election Commission leveled a $375,000 fine against President Barack Obama's 2008 presidential campaign for failing to properly report almost $2 million in 2008 campaign contributions, along with other violations. No criminal prosecutions. Nobody went to jail.

In the case of President Trump's former national security adviser, Michael Flynn, who pled guilty to lying to the FBI, the special counsel recommends no jail time. Flynn, according to the filing, gave the probe "substantial assistance." The filing described Flynn as "one of the few people with long-term and firsthand insight" into Mueller's investigation. But did Flynn give evidence of a Trump "collusion" or conspiracy with Russia to win the election—the purpose the Mueller investigation? So far, the investigation has resulted in the convictions of several Trump associates. Not one of the convictions, however, has had anything to do with a Trump-Russian "collusion."

If the definition of a successful special counsel or special prosecutor is the number of convictions he or she obtains, then the Whitewater investigation into an allegedly crooked Arkansas real-estate deal and a crooked Little Rock bank was an unmitigated success. True, that probe's big targets, Bill and Hillary Clinton, were not charged, but the investigation resulted in 14 convictions, including the then-governor of Arkansas.

Webster Hubbell, Hillary Clinton's former law partner at Little Rock's Rose Law Firm, was convicted. Hubbell, at the beginning of the probe, held the No. 3 position in the Justice Department. He admitted to stealing from clients and partners of his law firm and pled guilty to mail fraud and tax evasion. He was sentenced to 21 months in prison. He was later indicted on an additional 18 charges after resigning from the DOJ. The New York Times reported: "Some money Hubbell received in 1994, for which the prosecutor said he did 'little or no work,' might have been given to discourage him from being more candid with investigators. ... Much of the income Hubbell received in 1994 came from contracts arranged by close friends and supporters of the Clintons, suggesting to investigators that Hubbell may have been given money to discourage him from cooperating with the Whitewater independent counsel's office."

James McDougal, Clinton friend and Whitewater business partner, operated Madison Guaranty Savings and Loan, the bank under investigation. Madison failed in 1989, costing taxpayers $60 million. McDougal was convicted of 18 felony counts related to bad loans made by his bank. After his conviction, McDougal agreed to cooperate with the special prosecutor.

Susan McDougal, James McDougal's former wife, was a partner in the Whitewater land deal and in Madison Guaranty. She was convicted of four felony fraud counts, but refused to cooperate with the Whitewater prosecutors. McDougal was sentenced to 18 months in jail on a civil contempt charge, but still has refused to answer questions before a grand jury. She was later charged with criminal contempt and obstruction of justice. President Clinton gave her a full pardon in the final hours of his presidency.

Hillary Clinton called her husband a victim of a "vast right-wing conspiracy." Bill Clinton adviser Paul Begala called independent counsel Ken Starr "corrupt" and his investigation a "witch hunt" and "a scuzzy investigation" based on "leaks and lies and manufactured evidence." Clinton senior strategist Rahm Emanuel complained of the "partisan pursuit of the president." The difference is that the Whitewater convictions, as opposed to the Mueller probe convictions at this point, specifically related to the purpose of the probe.

Clearly, some Trump associates broke laws, and real-estate developer Trump perhaps made misleading statements about a proposed deal for a real-estate project in Russia. But since virtually every political pundit predicted Trump's landslide defeat in 2016, why the surprise that Trump was simultaneously working on his next act? As for the accusation that Trump directed Cohen to make payments to prevent his relationships with Daniels and McDougal from coming to light during the campaign, what happened to the Bill Clinton defense—"Everybody lies about sex"? Trump critics simultaneously called him an idiot and the conductor of a scheme intended to break campaign finance laws by using his own money to pay off mistresses.

The Department of Justice's Office of Legal Counsel, in 2000, wrote, "The indictment or criminal prosecution of a sitting President would unconstitutionally undermine the capacity of the executive branch to perform its constitutionally assigned functions." The recourse is impeachment and then removal from office, following a trial in the Senate. Unless the Mueller report contains a lot more than what we know, so far, neither is likely.

Gov. Jerry 'Moonbeam' Brown's Warning to Fellow Democrats

December 20, 2018

Outgoing California Gov. Jerry Brown recently said, "The weakness of the Republican Party has let the Democratic Party, I think, go get further out than I think the majority of people want." When a tax-spend-and-regulate Democrat who signed legislation making California the first "sanctuary state" says the Democrats have gotten too "further out" for the majority, that party would be wise to take notice. In the November elections, California Democrats won veto-proof supermajorities in both chambers of state government. No Republican currently holds an elected state-wide office.

Brown seems to recognize that there are only so many "rich" people and that one does become rich by being too stupid to know that the rich have options. California has the highest state income tax in the country, with a top marginal rate of 13.3 percent. Even left-wing, Trump-hating California resident Bill Maher complained about the state's high income taxes in 2013: "In California, I just want to say: Liberals, you could actually lose me. ... Rich people ... actually do pay the freight in this country ... like 70 percent" of the taxes.

As to who bears responsibility for the Democratic lurch to the left, Brown blames *Republican* "weakness." Follow that? Republican "weakness" practically forced the Democrats to pursue a hard-left agenda: abolishing Immigration and Customs Enforcement and pursuing "Medicare-for-all," $15 minimum wage, tuition-free college, and climate change alarmism.

Brown is warning the Democrats that President Donald Trump's agenda is closer to what Americans want than that of Alexandria Ocasio-Cortez, the House's newly elected self-described socialist. And

Brown is looking at results. Even the international community is grudgingly acknowledging the merits of Trump's positions.

Take, for instance, Trump's actions against China over the country's theft of intellectual property and the forced transfer of proprietary technology as a condition of doing business. Nicolas Chapuis, the EU ambassador of China, also recently sounded downright Trumpian while complaining of this practice: "This has to stop or to be regulated ... so that there is no so-called 'forced tech transfer.'"

The Europeans are echoing Trump's concerns about Iran that caused the U.S. to withdraw form the Iran deal. "Not only does the deal fail to halt Iran's nuclear ambitions," Trump said in explaining the withdrawal, "but it also fails to address the regime's development of ballistic missiles that could deliver nuclear warheads." Three weeks ago, Iran again test-fired a medium-range missile, capable of carrying multiple warheads and striking anywhere in the Middle East and parts of Europe. This alarmed the U.K., Germany and France, whose foreign ministry said, "(France) condemns this provocative and destabilizing action."

As for climate change, France's Emmanuel Macron lectured Trump last year on the risk of pulling out of the Paris climate agreement. Macron warned, "There is no Plan B because there is no Planet B." But Macron recently discovered a Plan B when, after days of riots in France, he agreed to suspend an unpopular climate-change gas tax that would have raised France's average price per gallon to nearly $8. In America, polls consistently rank climate change among Americans' least concerns.

As for the Democrats' push for "single-payer" health care, "Medicare-for-all" or "Sanders care," Ocasio-Cortez claims it can be paid for by ending the waste, fraud and abuse in our defense budget. The price tag for "Medicare-for-all" is generally estimated, by the Mercatus Center at George Mason University, to cost $32.6 trillion over 10 years. This year, the *entire* defense budget is under $700 billion. This leaves Ocasio-Cortez just a little short.

Brown senses the danger his party faces because of its blatant contempt for Trump. Mika Brzezinski, a co-host of MSNBC's "Morning Joe," criticized Secretary of State Mike Pompeo for, in her view, irresponsibly following Trump's lead in refusing to directly implicate Saudi Crown Prince Mohammed bin Salman in the murder of a

Washington Post Saudi columnist. Brzezinski said: "Why doesn't Mike Pompeo care? ... Are the pathetic deflections that we just heard ... is that a patriot speaking? Or a wannabe dictator's butt boy?"

Two days later—she was off the following day—Brzezinski gave this on-air apology: "I wanted to address a term that I used on this show on Wednesday that was vulgar. ... The term is crass and offensive, and I apologize to everybody, especially the LGBTQ community and to my colleagues for using it. It was a mistake. My father would have found it so unbecoming and disrespectful, and he would have told me. I will work hard to be better. But I just want to say on camera, looking viewers straight in the eye: I am really, really sorry." Notice anything missing? Brzezinski offered no direct apology to the target of her scorn—Pompeo himself. There is a term for this: "Trump Derangement Syndrome."

Brown, now that he's leaving office, feels free to speak his mind. He offers his party some advice. Countering Trump with Sanders care, "free" college tuition and abolishing ICE is not the road to victory in 2020.

About the Author

A "firebrand libertarian" according to Daily Variety, Larry Elder is a bestselling author, radio and TV talk show host with a take-no-prisoners style, using such old-fashioned things as evidence and logic. Larry shines the bright light of reasoned analysis on many of the myths and hypocrisies apparent in our government, our society and our media. He slays dragons and topples sacred cows with facts, common sense and a ready wit.

Larry hosted the longest-running afternoon drive-time radio show in Los Angeles for 15 years, beginning in March 1994. "The Larry Elder Show," a top-rated daily program on KABC 790, became a nationally syndicated daily talk show for ABC Radio Networks on Aug. 12, 2002. Known to his listeners as the "Sage From South Central," Larry sizzles on the airwaves with his thoughtful insight on the day's most provocative issues, to the delight, consternation and entertainment of his listeners.

In his bestselling book "The 10 Things You Can't Say in America," Larry skewers the crippling myths that dominate the public agenda. Larry punctures all pretension, trashes accepted "wisdom" and puts everyone on notice that the status quo must be shaken up. In his second book, "Showdown: Confronting Bias, Lies and the Special Interests That Divide America," Larry again takes on the nanny state, the "victicrats" and the politically correct. His latest book, "What's Race Got to Do with It? Why It's Time to Stop the Stupidest Argument in America," is being praised as a groundbreaking must-read for the future of race relations in America. Elder also writes a nationally syndicated newspaper column distributed by Creators Syndicate.

Larry was also host of the television shows "Moral Court" and "The Larry Elder Show." Larry created, directed and produced the film "Michael & Me," a documentary that examines gun use in America.

The New Trump Standard
is also available as an e-book
for Kindle, Amazon Fire, iPad, Nook and
Android e-readers. Visit
creatorspublishing.com to learn more.

o o o

CREATORS PUBLISHING

We publish books.
We find compelling storytellers and
help them craft their narrative,
distributing their novels and collections
worldwide.

o o o

Made in the USA
Coppell, TX
16 August 2020